WITCHCRAFT, THE OCCULT
AND HOW TO
SELECT A FAMILIAR

A SHAMAN'S PERSONAL WORKBOOK AND STUDY GUIDE

By Maria D'Andrea

Contributors:
Rick Holecek
Rob D'Andrea
Artwork by Mark Taylor

YES YOU CAN SERIES

WITCHCRAFT, THE OCCULT AND HOW TO SELECT A FAMILIAR

A SHAMAN'S PERSONAL WORKBOOK AND STUDY GUIDE

Earl, The Proud Familiar of April Troiani and Tim Beckley.

Deceased April 2019 With Loving Affection.

ABOUT THE AUTHOR

Maria D'Andrea is an internationally known professional psychic from Budapest, Hungary. Since early childhood she has demonstrated high spiritual awareness and psychic ability.

Over her lifetime and as a Spiritual Leader, she has provided excellent psychic guidance and enlightenment to many people, assisting them on their own personal path of spiritual self discovery. Many occultists and psychics specialize in only one area, for example Tarot card reading or Psychometry. When you work with Maria, you can rest assured that she will be able to use the best method to achieve the best results for your particular circumstance.

Maria is known for a unique form of divination called "Rune Casting." This method was used by Vikings and Europeans to unlock information about the past, present and future by tapping into the Universal Mind. The responsibility of a selection of paths is yours after you have been made aware of the underlying factors and forces at work.

WITCHCRAFT, THE OCCULT AND HOW TO SELECT A FAMILIAR

A Shaman's Personal Workbook and Study Guide

Maria D' Andrea

INNER LIGHT/GLOBAL COMMUNICATIONS

P.O. Box 753
New Brunswick, NJ 08903

mrufo8@hotmail.com

Witchcraft, The Occult And How To Select A Familiar A Shaman's Personal Workbook and Study Guide
©By Maria D'Andrea

Copyright © 2019 by Timothy Green Beckley dba
Inner Light/Global Communications

Published in the United States of America by Inner Light/Global Communications, PO Box 753 - New Brunswick, NJ 08903

Staff Members:

Timothy G. Beckley, Publisher

Carol Ann Rodriguez, Assistant to the Publisher

Sean Casteel, General Associate Editor

Tim R. Swartz, Formatting, Graphics and Editorial Consultant

William Kern, Editorial and Art Consultant

www.ConspiracyJournal.com

Order Hot Line: 1-732-602-3407

PayPal: MrUFO8@hotmail.com

OTHER BOOKS BY MARIA D'ANDREA

Secret Occult Gallery And Spell Casting Formulary

You Can Take It With You: Paying Your Way Into God's Higher Kingdom

Occult Grimoire And Magical Formulary

Secret Magical Elixirs Of Life

Miracle Candle Spells: With Candle Burning Prayers For A Good And Prosperous Life

Your Personal Mega Power Spells - For Love, Luck, Prosperity

Angel Spells: The Enochian Occult Workbook Of Charms, Seals, Talismans And Ciphers

Simple Spells With Playing Cards

Maria D' Andrea's Positively Positive Spell Book

Mythical, Magickal Beasts And Beings

The Complete Magickal, Spiritual And Occult Oils Workbook From A-Z

How To Eliminate Stress And Anxiety Through The Occult

100% Positive Spells And Incantations For Aladdin's Magick Lamp

Heaven Sent Money Spells - Divinely Inspired For Your Wealth

<u>Yes You Can Series</u>

Evocation: Evoke the Power of Inter-dimensional Beings

The Sexy Medium's Love and Lust Spells

Travel The Waves of Time: Contacting Beneficial Beings

Supernatural Words of Power

Maria D' Andrea's Book of Common Prayer

DEDICATION

To my son, Rick Holecek: Who has always walked the Warrior Path of Light.

To my son, Rob D'Andrea: Who has a magickal touch in all he endeavors to do.

I thank you both for always being there for me and being the wonderful men that you are. We have traveled this realm with love, adventure and insight together. As always -You are my greatest gifts.

CONTENTS

Maria D'Andrea

FOREWORD

By Robert D'Andrea

I would like to start off by saying that Maria D'Andrea has given us another fantastic book. She has perfected the art of taking a vast subject and breaking it down to the essentials. Whether this is your introduction to familiars or you are already knowledgeable about this topic, I guarantee that you will get a lot out of this book and will be able to use it as a reference in the future..

This book isn't just educational, it is fun to read. You will learn about what familiars are as well as their main purpose, and you will also learn how they are used in different cultures and religions...Familiars are used in magick by magi, witches, occultists, shamans and many, many more. The main reason I pick Maria D'Andrea's books to read for any metaphysical or spiritual topics that I am interested in is because they teach me the concepts as well as the particulars.

I know you will enjoy this book as much as I did, and I advise you to read other books by Maria D'Andrea to bring you up to speed on her other topics. You will gain so much information that you will be able to participate in conversations about these topics. On top of that you will have an understanding about these subjects.

CHAPTER ONE

A SHAMAN SPEAKS

I am originally from Budapest, Hungary. My heritage is that of the Magyar/Hun nations. I have spent all my life living in both worlds of man and spirit. This is a part of my journey, my story and my trust in God/Divine Power that's carried me through. I am thankful that I can share knowledge with you, so you can consciously use your free will to improve upon your life.

As a child, my mother and I escaped during the Hungarian Revolution. She told me that at one point, the group we were with didn't know if they should go forward or go back. They stopped for a short time to discuss it. She said I told the group that God told me if we move forward we would be safe and protected. Part of the group decided to go back. Others asked me some questions and decided to move forward. My mother said that the things I said were obviously not something a six year old would say or know. Unfortunately, we heard later through the underground that all the people in the group that went back were killed. We made it to freedom with everyone in the group surviving.

I always knew that walking the shamanic path was what I was meant to do and who I am.

There is a thin line, a tightrope of sorts that we walk on. One side is this realm of the physical and the other side is the spiritual realms. We can control which Path we are on and how to work with them. I always say I only work the positive side. I believe that what you do (good, bad or indifferent) will come back to you. I tune into our Source (whatever name you call your source is what works for you) for information, clarity and guidance. I've said I Go Direct so often, that one of my students, Rodney, started saying "IGD."

It doesn't matter what system you utilize to gain an outcome, as long as it is positive, harms none and it resonates with you.

I find that I use whatever system works for that particular situation, on the positive side. This can be witchcraft, paganism, Christianity, Shamanism from any culture, among other styles.

This also includes Christian formulae that people don't connect normally to the occult/metaphysics. As an example: the churches have incense (as we do), they light candles for those who passed or for other personal reasons (again, as we do) and they do invocation (as do we). They have their own ceremonies (need I say?).

All cultures down through the centuries have utilized occult magick. Occult simply means ancient wisdom, hidden knowledge. It is understanding nature to work with those tremendous forces to gain success in your life. Now they refer to it as metaphysics or paranormal. Whatever name you wish to call it, it's still occult. Magick is considered an ancient art and science. Chemistry came out of alchemy (a chemist will tell you that), physics came out of metaphysics (occult). Magick is really the oldest science

Some shaman, witches, magi, wizards, high priestesses, light workers and others work in secrecy, while some work in the open, helping others or helping themselves and those close to them with a smile.

We work with the Invisible Laws and can harness energy, send it out, have a direct link with our Source. We can work alone or call familiars and deities and other sources to work with us. You have to love that we have free will.

At times we are like chameleons, blending in with society with secrecy in order not to disclose our abilities. Sometimes we are warriors, protectors, spiritual leaders, healers, shaman, medicine people, occultists and more. Some of us are out in the open about who we are and what we do. Neither way is good or bad, it is simply a free will choice at the time.

As a European Shaman, you have to have knowledge and the ability to work with many abilities, not just one. If you think in terms of ancient times, such as tribal, you'll get a better sense of what we really do. As an example: we are the religious leaders of the tribe/society (I'm an interfaith minister), you need to be able to counsel (I'm a pastoral counselor), to do healing for those who need it (I'm a healer), to do prophecy (I'm a professional psychic). The reason for the psychic part is because the tribes were nomadic, so they needed to know what direction to travel where there's water, not to go where there's quicksand, what the chances are of victory in battle and how to proceed to improve the outcome, among other issues. You also needed to know weapons (both physical and spiritual) to protect the tribe (I'm versed in several types in both physical and non-physical) and you need to be a master with magick. We also pass on the knowledge to those who are ready (I'm an author and teacher in the psychic /spiritual/occult fields) and the Founder of several enlightenment mystery schools/groups.

I am merely letting you know who I am, so you understand why I have this knowledge and where all this information is coming from to be of help to you. It has been passed down through the centuries and much of this knowledge is also developed by me.

*** If you are reading this book, then you are ready to move forward in accomplishing your intent.

So as you can see, there's more to it than people realize.

We are all intertwined with nature. It seems people forget this at times. Now is the time to work with nature outside of ourselves and within ourselves.

Nature is all around us. It seems that some people think of nature in terms of going somewhere that has a pristine natural environment. You can ask any scientist, that place doesn't exist. Spores flow from one place to another, the wind carries seeds, water that has fish or animals bathing in it and drinking from it has already been altered and it comes down river to towns and so it goes.

When you are in the cities, there are parks, nature preserves, trees, birds, animals and so much more. You just have to start looking around you and appreciating nature that is already near you. If I hike on the paths near my home or in the Catskill Mountains, either way, I'm in nature.

Familiars are also part of nature. They are all forms of energy, whether in a physical form or in the etheric planes, just like us. You will be able to connect with your familiars so they can assist you in achieving your goals, making your life better, having more clarity and gaining power over your future, instead of others and society having power over your life. After all, it's your future that we are talking about.

Let's get a better understanding of how this works, what to do and to forge forward to achieve your dreams. You are an unlimited spirit in a physical body. Remember who YOU are. You are a co-creator. You will come to see and feel your power. Your potential is already there. We need to simply ignite that spark within.

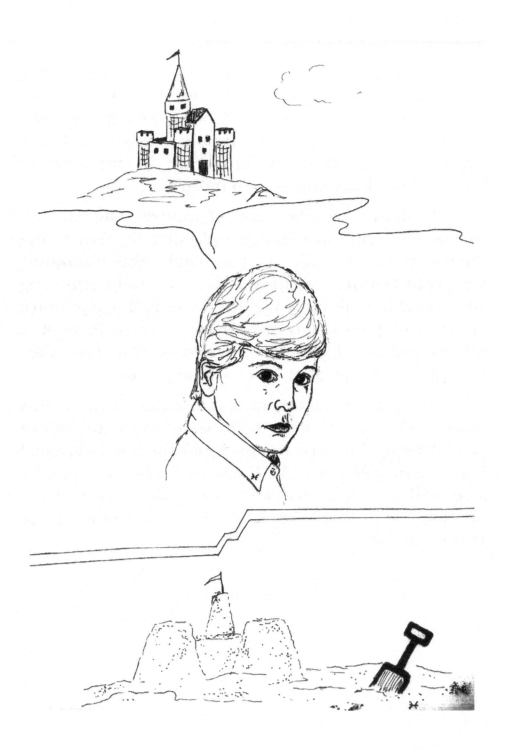

CHAPTER TWO
WORKING CONCEPTS

Let's get acquainted with unlocking your potential. It is in you. I will help you to find the key to open your door. To make that shift in your consciousness to recognize who you are and what you can achieve and create.

As with any other form of knowledge, without the concepts of what you are about to embark upon, you will not be able to work with your familiars or to gain the desired outcome you are about to manifest on the level that you can truly achieve. Remember, the only limitations you have are the ones you set for yourself. Stop thinking in the third dimensional view and look at all the miracles around you. Some things just don't make sense in how they can even exist, yet, there they are.

You are one of those miracles. There is only one of you. You are a unique creation of your Source of nature. There will never be another one of you in this whole universe, in the physical or in the spiritual realms. Think how special that makes you.

Now, I know some of you will have a difficult time seeing yourself this way because of previous feedback and the actions of others around you. You may have had negative relatives, friends, co-workers who made you question yourself. You are going to let that go now. You will remind yourself each morning upon awakening that you are a special, unique being and you don't have any limits put on you by others.

As they say, you can't change the past, be happily aware of your present and what is happening in it, whatever you are focused on now is setting into motion what will come to you in the future, so be conscious of your thoughts and actions as much as possible.

Whenever you have a negative thought (this won't work, I'll never get better, I've never been able to do that, I'll never be able to make enough money, I'm always unlucky, I'll never have the relationship I'd like, I'm not smart enough, I don't look the way I'd like...), think of the word "Cancel" and rephrase your thought to either the opposite (I can do this...) or simply substitute a positive thought (a wonderful memory, a vacation you'd like to go on, a goal you will achieve or even a dinner you are looking forward to having).

There are days when I walk around going "Cancel," "Cancel," "Cancel." We all have those days. It's not that we are avoiding those days; it's that we are able to handle them better and not play into the negative aspects to keep them going. If you never have a bad day, you are probably not human...I always look for the best (it doesn't mean I'm unaware of the negative, I just pick my focus). Of course, there are days that I think God looks down on me and just laughs and laughs and laughs.

There is an occult Law that states that wherever our thoughts go, that's how our future will be because we are creating it. We've all known someone that says they have a headache all the time. Then when they get one, they're the only ones who are surprised. We knew it was coming. If you focus on the negative, you get negative. If you focus on the positive, you get positive. Speak your truth.

We are in an energy stream and we need to be in that flow. Relax and let yourself flow with ease in the direction you consciously picked. You're streaming energy toward your intent. What are you manifesting your future to be? If you like your direction, stay on that path. If you don't like where your future is heading, change your direction.

You're sitting on a moving train. Do you want to stay on it or change to a different train?

Anchor yourself into your goal, into the destination in your life.

Change your outlook to change your life. That's the bottom line.

Whatever you are working on, you need to act, think, feel, and dress the part as if you've already achieved it. Feel like you've already been victorious. If you want a higher position in the company, dress as if you're going to work in that position today, and be self-confident and happy. If you are creating more money and you're considering buying something small (not like a car), spend the money happily, as if you have all the money you're creating, then it will come. When I was starting out manifesting in my teens, I actually spent more money while manifesting for extra money, as if I already had more abundance.

We are never defeated. Our Source wants us to thrive and be happy. We just have to pick our Path.

Ask yourself, when something doesn't work, are you willing to get back up?

Abraham Lincoln had an unbelievable number of goals which weren't successful. He kept getting back up, tried different ways and different goals, and after many unsuccessful ventures he became the President of the United States.

I never give up. If something doesn't work, I look for a different approach and refocus. Now, there are times in our lives when something is just not meant to be. You have to see it, look at what you learned from it and know when to move on.

We are beings of desire. Desire and curiosity is a driving force. We as humans are constantly seeking to improve the conditions in our lives. That is a positive force. If you didn't desire anything, can you imagine what your life would be like? You wouldn't have goals and nothing would change by your choice. Outside forces would still cause changes but you'd be more like a feather in the wind with no direction. Now, your desire doesn't have to be life altering, it could be that you desire tickets to a sporting event or to a show. Desire and curiosity is how we discovered fire. This is how the airplane came into being, as well as computers.

We've heard of people who made so much money that they retired early, thinking they don't need to work anymore. Then you hear how they are depressed, tired and frustrated. Now, you may wonder how this can be since they've obviously reached their goal. It's simple; they have nothing to look forward to. They are now inactive. They may go on vacations and buy new cars, but that will wear off. They no longer have a destination and will feel, many times, that they are at the end of the line (not literally) with nothing exciting to look forward to. And most will go back to work or volunteer in some way, but they will find a new desire to work toward to feel energized, useful and happy again.

Although we have a destination, remember to let yourself experience the journey and have fun. Sometimes the journey is the exciting part. Once you've achieved your desire, pick a new one. It can be something day to day, like reading a particular book or seeing a movie. Once you've done that, set a new goal to keep yourself in motion. (That doesn't mean we don't take breaks.)

Take some time to think about it. What is your main desire? In this case, which familiar can you call to you to help move things quicker?

A client's story—

As an example: one of my students, Larry (not his real name), was in a limiting job. He was working in an office doing the same thing each day. He'd always be bored. Larry would quit or set himself up to be fired. On to the next job. He would reach a top level in his new job and get frustrated or bored because there was nowhere else to move up. Again he'd quit or get fired. The pattern kept repeating, not because Larry couldn't do the job, but because he was in the wrong type of job for himself.

He put a call out to have a familiar come to him, in a way that he will have no doubt that this is his sign which will help point the way he should go. For the next few days, he constantly kept seeing birds flying. On TV, more than the normal amount on the streets, even in advertisements. He thought about what birds meant to him and realized it meant they had freedom to go where they chose, and that also meant to Larry that they were flexible.

Larry was meant to be in a flexible job.

He ended up seeing the issue and took a job as a manager. Larry can now make decisions and doesn't have to always sit in one place. He's had the job now for over 16 years and is very happy. He found his answer by finding who his familiars were at that time. That told him what qualities he had at the moment. You have to know when to make changes/improvements in your life. It could also be that he simply outgrew that type of job through time or through changes in his personality and the familiar pointed this out to him.

* * * * * *

We have all heard various tales, myths, legends and recognize many of them. However, some are stories, some are based in truth and some are truths that we work with. We are not focused here on truth according to society, but truth that comes from knowing and already working truth in both realms.

Consciously and with the Rights as a spiritual being, you can incorporate these truths into your life to not just exist, but to make your future better. Do you realize that you're already walking on a path to your future? Of course you are. Now, you can decide if you wish to stay on the path you're now creating or if you are going to create a new, different path. Hmmm. Decisions, decisions, decisions...But they can be fun.

The unknown future isn't to be dismissed, it is to be looked at and worked with. Yay, woo hoo, new opportunities.

We all make mistakes. Have you looked at humanity lately? It's normal. Sometimes it's even funny. We laugh, move on and look at how we can make things work.

We work with cause and effect. We are the oldest science. If we repeat a formula/spell and it works with the same outcome every time, we will pass it down through our families and others who are ready. If we don't get the same outcome, we simply stop doing it. After all, why pass on a hit and miss formulae? I always say: it's like repeating your grandmother's recipe exactly because everyone loved it. It will always have the same happy results. If we decide to adjust/ tweak it to make it better or different, others may or may not like it, but it definitely won't be the same as your grandmothers.

There are many dimensions. Be open to the realms you cannot see, touch or feel in this physical plane. I always say to my students: it is like electricity. We don't see it, but we don't put our fingers in the socket.

***Zen Master Huang-Po said:

"On seeing one thing, you see all things...when you see a grain of sand, you see all possible worlds, with all their vast rivers and mountains. When you see a drop of water you see the nature of all the waters of the universe."

This is also known as the holographic concept in science. Be open to mystical experiences.

Remember above all else that you have these abilities through your Source. God, Great Spirit, Divine Power or whatever name fits with your particular belief system. When I write the word God, as an example, substitute the name you normally connect with to make it personal and powerful.

It is not where you are today; it is where you are going. And that is where your focus leads you. So be a guardian at the gate of your thoughts. Pay attention and once in a while mentally step back and look to see what your thoughts were throughout the day. Are they in sync with your goals? No? Then change them.

Look at your environment and be around people who win in a positive way.

It is important to have no doubt, no doubt. You're getting help from your familiar, so you have "back up."

Of course, there are challenges. After all, we are human and learning how to navigate the waters of life. We are interconnected with nature. Some of us are aware, some not. We are not in the business of converting others, we are working on ourselves to improve our lives and elevate ourselves on a spiritual level. We can help others and impact their lives in a positive way at times, but we cannot elevate their souls, only our own. Can we all see that?

There are extra-dimensions of realities. You are a small part of it and because you are connected to these, you are able to link up to familiars. You can tap into various levels of consciousness and spread your wings to fly in any direction/path of your choosing to form the future you envision.

You are at a milestone point. You will not move ahead unless your mindset changes from your everyday, mundane outlook to that of a spiritual being of power. Each spiritual level moves you up as you climb the ladder of awakening, knowledge and abilities. This is the time to walk the Path of Light. Take flight within your soul and be in harmony with nature and with your familiars.

CHAPTER THREE
WHAT ARE FAMILIARS FOR THOSE THAT AREN'T FAMILIAR

First, you should remember that working with familiars isn't limited by time and space. Those are manmade outlooks to help us function in the physical plane and do not exist in the realms we will be journeying on.

The bottom line is this:

A familiar can be on the physical or non-physical plane and is basically one that you have a psychic link with and who will help you in a magickal way by choice.

They have to work with us by their choice. And of course, by our choice. We never restrict them. We have a psychic link to our familiar and have to respect it. A psychic link is very serious. We don't want that connection to anything negative on either side of reality. By the way, a familiar is never a person.

Thinking of familiars brings forth a vision of cats by a cauldron and a witch, mainly because of past misconceptions and of course the media. Although familiars are used in what people think of as harmful witchcraft, they seem to forget it's also used in helping with healing, relationships, prosperity and so forth. Nature is neutral. The person doing magick is positive or negative, not nature.

I always say, if there's a drought and it rains, that is positive. Now, if your neighbor is building an ark, not so much. But the rain itself is neutral; our perspective makes it good or bad.

Part of the shamanic outlook of old is that the more connections you have the more power you have. However, that isn't necessarily the case. That was partly based on magi fighting war against other magi. Usually this meant positive and negative energies in battle. Battle in this form can cause physical death on this plane. Of course, there are negative, harmful, dangerous entities. It's not that we are unaware of them; it is just that we don't allow them in. I know I'm repeating this, but we truly ONLY do positive, we work in the Light.

***I am always saying it's imperative to utilize some form of psychic self-defense before you sojourn into unknown territory. This will keep you safe. Anything positive can still work with you. Anything harmful will be kept at bay and unable to get to you.

I give you one of my techniques which you can utilize in the section on *Finding Your Connections*.

Your familiar has to fit your lifestyle, be dedicated to you which means there's a psychic bond between you and it has abilities that you can call on or/and that are already within you. Abilities are usually both types.

People in all cultures connect with familiars. You are either positive or negative. There aren't gray areas. Think of it like this: it's either raining or it is not. There is an occult law that states: like attracts like.

Thus, knowing which familiar joins you, you will see parts of who you are. Makes you go hmmmm?

*** Familiars are physical and/or non-physical beings. Some other names for familiars are totems, guardians, spirit animals, physical animals, elementals, elves, fairies, leprechauns, dragons, unicorns, Pegasus, astral dwellers, ancestors (including parents), spirit teachers, ghosts, angels, insects, air/sea/land animals, imps, protectors, advisors, path finder (for finding your path) and many more.

Also there are stones, trees and herbs. These connections are also considered familiars.

These have the accumulation of all their species' abilities and qualities. Much like the holographic universe, one part has all the other parts contained within it.

Remember, life is an adventure.

You are in the process of awakening to wonderful realms, power and possibilities.

You aren't going to work hard on money or love, among other situations. When you know and trust and do the plan, everything will simply come. You are only working on: gaining technique/formulae, on knowing, respect (for your familiars), and trust.

In essence when working with a familiar, I am/we are the spirit animal. They blend with us at the time.

Story—

At one time, one of my familiars was a deer. I was on a hike by myself in the mountains, and I had the urge to look over to my right. When I looked, I saw a deer a few feet away from me just standing still and staring at me. The deer was comfortable with me, sensing I won't harm it and feeling I had a connection to it. (Animals are very sensitive to danger and/or safety.)

It was funny, because we just stood there a few minutes staring at each other, neither one of us moving. As I looked, I felt like I was being drawn out of my body and toward the deer. All of a sudden I was inside the deer, feeling my new body shape, and looking out at the mountain through its eyes. The funny thing was that everything I saw was gray, white or dark. Nothing had color. That was a surprise. I spent a few minutes like that, seeing out of its eyes.

Just as suddenly, I was back in my body looking, once again at the deer. I thanked it and it slowly walked away.

You really can't make this stuff up...

Their job is to help you gain your intent. They aid you to move you up in life. We only do so in a positive way. After all, we don't want to be around when the repercussions hit, unless they're positive ones, right? Remember Karma (what you put out, you get back) is a real and an active force.

Get excited about new opportunities because they're coming.

You have a job folding-a better one is coming, can't pay the rent-they'll help you and it'll be covered or you'll get a better one, your friendship folds – you've outgrown it and another one more suited to you is coming. God moves in mysterious ways and familiars are helpers to move you upward.

You are a powerful being. You have conscious control because we, as humans, have free will.

When you connect to your familiar, they become a part of you. They are power animals or powerful familiars in whatever form they show up. They come to you because you have some type of rapport. They are sacred beings.

They have to want to work with you. They can't be forced or coerced. They have to choose you too. Remember that it is a partnership.

If it's any form of animal, it connects to the animal qualities within you.

Familiars can be fun, have a sense of humor, be serious, mischievous, practical, playful, informative, loving, guiding, protecting. They bring awareness and truth to your life.

They help elevate you spiritually, as well as, connecting you with nature, other realms and magick.

They can inspire you and work with you in amazing ways.

Many witches, occultists, wizards, high priestesses, shamans, among other experts in their fields have familiars they either have with them, close to them or ones they can call upon at will.

Witches, shaman and occultist may call on their familiar through rituals. All cultures have magick, and those who have mastered it. This can be done outside or inside, depending on the ritual itself. Although after a period of time, some can be called forth directly. Much depends on your personal choice and the link between you.

These connections may be for a specific situation, ongoing for years or a lifetime.

As a side note, some totems are connected to tribes, nations or any group that may be formed in society. As a quick example, the legend as it has been kept by oral tradition in the Hungarian (Magyar) nation is that we have a bird called Turul. This bird is mythical and it is said that when the nation or when someone Hungarian is in trouble, they can call on the Turul and it will come to help. In America you have the eagle. And so it goes. In this book, we are only focused on the totems that work with us as individual people.

They have been used in several religions, as help in being a gateway to the Source for guidance and information. The Delphi oracle, who was connected to the spirit world, some say also through a connection to other worldly help, was sought after for knowledge to know ahead of time if a war was coming, who would win and if there was anything they could do to prevent it or make it a better outcome for their society. The oracle could be called upon also for mundane matters in business, health or in matters of love.

You need to be aware these are not pets. A familiar is your partner, although you have the control, since we have free will. Both of you are in tune with each other and there is a balance between you. You need to have respect and acknowledge the synchronistic levels that brought you together.

Unless you are working on a specific situation and called forth a particular spirit to help you, it is more important that they find you rather than you find them. Which goes back to - telling you something about yourself, possibly your qualities, who you are and/or what abilities you already possess. (Or can gain.) These ancient ties continue because they work.

Familiars are considered supernatural entities that aid us in our quests. Supernatural is really natural to us. Let me give you an example I use in teaching my classes and at seminars: if you wear glasses, you are being supernatural. This is because your normal vision might be limited. This is your natural limited vision. Enhancing it with glasses is past your natural ability and therefore super (past) natural. Gives you a different insight, right?

At times, a familiar works for a witch or shaman to help in a multitude of endeavors or chores (like a spirit dog or a physical dog barking at a negative intruder as a warning to be on y our guard).

Cats are frequent familiars with witches and others. One of the reasons is that they are more self-reliant so you can be away at work, in the woods, on a hike or away anywhere and they can take care of themselves having more independent energy than a fish who you'd have to make sure is always fed and taken care of if you're on a trip. Of course, depending on you and your lifestyle, a fish may be perfect for you.

Make sure you have a connection to your familiar. If you decide to get one on the physical plane and you're only getting one to work with because taking care of it is convenient, it won't work out for you. It may become a pet but not a familiar.

Remember, there will be a psychic link. This connection will be on a deeper and deeper level. You need to be careful who/what you build that link with.

This is not a game.

Familiars are all some form of magickal beings. They have a psychic link to you and are in harmony with who you are, what you do and how you live. Remember they are attracted to the "real" you. We are back to like attracts like.

Have you ever noticed that, as an example, you being a positive spiritual being, will automatically, without thought, be uncomfortable around people or animals that are negative? They will also be uncomfortable around you. This is just fine, since you wouldn't want to be around them more then you need to. After all, we can't avoid people in some situations involving relatives or business.

Story—

I had a powerful vision. I was sitting in my living room and doing some focused shamanic work. I felt I had a new familiar and wanted to know what it was.

As I sat there relaxed, I realized I was feeling my body energetically shift and change. It felt like my hands grew longer and long sturdy nails extended from them. My ears grew and I felt I could hear sounds farther away. As I sat there, my whole body, a step at a time, shifted into something other than me, yet still me. My spirit didn't change and I was completely aware, so I could stop it at any time I wanted to. In the end, I realized I shifted into a wolf. I felt perfectly relaxed, just checking out m y body mentally (without moving) and getting an idea of what traits connected to my wolf familiar. In this way, if I needed to call, I would already be aware of the abilities that he possessed.

When I felt I was finished, I only had to think about wanting to come back to myself and a little at a time, my energy reverted to being me again.

Familiars also, as I've mentioned, have a strong bond with you. It is an unconditional one. A connection that is very difficult to explain, but one you will feel intensely.

HOW TO TELL IF YOU HAVE ONE

This is something you need to be aware of so you don't misunderstand that a pet you love, a spirit such as an archangel or anything else you wish to be your familiar, really is one.

There is a difference. It is sometimes wishful thinking. Of course, a fairy can be "called in" to help you in your endeavor, but that doesn't make one a familiar.

So the question is...do you already have a familiar or will you gain one now?

This is the main difference:

You saw a cute cat in a store, it was adorable. Looked cuddly and you bought it and took it home. That's great but it doesn't make the kitty a familiar.

Now, you are walking by a pet shop. You don't have any intention of getting any type of pet. Yet, as you walk by, you have a strong urge to stop. You keep walking anyway. The feeling is so strong that you have to turn around and go back, just to get it out of your mind and to get rid of that feeling. You go back and look around, nothing interests you. You turn a corner and you have an instant affinity to a particular cat. The cat seems to stare back and it feels like you have a link with each other. You just "know" you can't leave it there and subsequently take it home. This kitten is your familiar. It will be loyal to you, help you grow spiritually and help you in many other ways. One of them is if you're in danger, the kitten will warn you by its actions. So pay attention.

On another note, you might go to museums frequently. When you consciously think of it, you realize you are always attracted to the section on Native Americans and mainly to the turquoise gemstones. This tells you that your connection is that particular stone. Turquoise is an all-purpose stone and it contains the energies for healing, luck, protection, spirituality and prosperity. If you decide to carry it or wear it, those are the situations it will attract to you.

Along the same line, if you go to the zoo or are simply attracted to pictures of a particular animal consistently, such as a wolf or penguin, this also tells you that you have that connection.

It can also be a mythical creature. Many are "real" on the astral plane.

Story—

My spiritual brother, Francis Revesl-Bey and I were driving home late one night from upstate New York. We just finished doing Readings at the Renaissance Fair and discussing how beautiful and warm it was out. How we loved connecting to nature in all its beauty.

All of a sudden as we were about to get onto the parkway leading home, I had a very strong urge to slow down. At the same time, he said he felt a deer and we should slow down because it was close, which we naturally did.

As we rounded the turn for the parkway ramp, there was the deer, just standing in the middle of the road, in the dark. If we were going the normal speed, we would have hit it. It just stared at us and slowly went on its way.

That doesn't make the deer a familiar connection to us. We were just more aware on the energy plane of the different realms and trusted it enough to move on it. So trust your intuitive nature.

Through time, I've found that my sons and I can send spirits, feelings or thoughts back and forth. At times it's just fun and saying hi or "hey, call me when you can. Not a rush." In an emergency we will feel it more directly on a psychic level or as much as we are magickal beings, we do pick up the phone and call.

After all, we live in both realities of man and spirit. We always work from both. If nothing else, humanity can be very versatile.

Remember, that though you walk both realms, you should be aware when you have to be serious and when you need to laugh. After all, have you seen the universe and all its unique forms? Tell me some of it isn't funny. You can't go to the zoo and be serious. Without a sense of humor, you really won't do as well. Some days I just laugh.

It makes me want to get out a cauldron, throw some herbs in it and a plastic snake and see what people think when they visit. Come on, you know it's funny.

The more you do positive magick, the more your sense of humor changes. Alright, I'll admit it gets a little warped sometimes, but that can be fun. After all, your familiars can use lightheartedness at times too.

A familiar can be on the physical or non-physical plane and is basically one that you have a psychic link with and who will help you in a magickal way by choice.

CHAPTER FOUR
FINDING YOUR CONNECTIONS

Alright, I know they aren't really lost. However, they have been lost to you. It's like going on a treasure hunt. Who or what you find will enrich your life and help you to reach the destination, the goals you set for yourself.

I will help you on your path to find your special familiar(s).

You are a spiritual warrior of light. You are entering a different realm, the extra-dimensional universe and beyond. And you don't even need a spaceship for your journey. How great is that?

You will need protection, knowledge, intent, focus, loyalty, self-confidence, desire, anticipation, knowing and gratitude.

This is an exciting time. Get excited. Be happy. Be expectant. Have gratitude. And have a sense of humor. (You will need it at times. You have to love the universe and its quirky self.) So...let's go.

These are the necessary essential qualities for achieving your goals and connecting to your familiar:

Protection - You have to know psychic self-defense in order to be safe. It doesn't matter if you use my method or a different form. As long as it works for you, that's all that counts. It will protect you 100% on the etheric side and about 95% on the physical side, because there are experiences we need to go through to learn in this lifetime. Knowing physical defense is also an added positive.

Knowledge – You can't achieve anything without the understanding of how it works and the knowledge of how to work with it. We are never above learning from whatever source will move us upward. We are always learning and expanding.

Intent – You have to have a goal to work toward. It doesn't have to always be something major. It can be simple and small. At times, we really don't have a goal. Then, as an example, the goal can be getting home early. As long as you pick a destination, you will get there. If you're in a boat and you didn't pick a shore to row toward, the current will take you wherever it wants to and that may not be where you want to end up. So consciously pick your intent. If you are neutral and don't pick, in essence you chose to have the current decide for you.

Focus – Without focus, you'll get lost. How many people do you know that had a goal last year but didn't stay focused on it and now they don't even remember what it was? When you come to a crossroad, stay focused on which road moves you to your destination. Your familiars will help you.

Loyalty – And so we come to loyalty. Your familiar will always be connected and loyal to you. In return you need to be loyal to your familiar.

Self-confidence – Part of self-confidence is to know what you are doing (knowledge, positive outlook, ability) from your training and experiences. This is not ego. This is awareness. You are a powerful source of Divine Energy. Look at how powerful your Source is. How can you possibly not have confidence in yourself, when Divine Power has given you part of Himself/Herself? You and your Source are one. You only need to remind yourself at times. I always explain it this way: One of the shamanic ways to look at it is that there is a gigantic sun. Each ray coming from the sun is a soul (you). Hence, you are part of your Source. When we say "I am God," this is what we mean. Not that we are THE One.

Desire – Without the flame of desire to move you, how will you get there? It is similar to a battery charger. Desire motivates you, keeps you on track, excites you and moves you in a happy direction.

Anticipation – There are two levels to this. The 1st is that you need to know what you're doing and as in chess, anticipate what the outcome will be depending on what actions or decisions you make. 2nd - If you are not expecting it to work and you aren't looking forward to it then why would it come to you? The universe will feel that energy and say - if it doesn't matter that much to (you)...then why do I need to hurry to bring it in? I can take my time or just not get to it since it's not important. You know you don't want that...Right?

Knowing – As you ask, you are already answered. You have to get used to that feeling of trust. Know that your Source wants you to succeed, to be happy. Your familiar will aid you in gaining your intent. Don't question it. You have to feel it in your heart that the outcome you are manifesting is coming to you. Know it as a fact. If you find you are questioning it, think or say "cancel" and replace it immediately with a positive thought. It takes time to develop this and doesn't come overnight on this level, but it is a key factor.

Gratitude – I tell my students in this manner - think of having an earthly father who took you to the store. While there, you asked him for candy. Your father replied that he will get it for you on the way out. And you immediately say "thank you." You know that the whole time in the store you are expecting the candy. You don't question if you'll get it since your father already said he would get it on the way out. But, you're excited and not questioning the results. However, you'll notice that you said "thank you" when he said he will get it. You didn't wait until you actually had it in your hand because you knew that when you asked and he said yes, it was already on its way. You just weren't sure when because he had shopping to do first. That's the grateful attitude you have to have. Your Source and your familiar will work at helping you in gaining your goals.

You are at the gates of the universe, let the positive in. Decide to walk through the gate and open up your spirit, mind and heart.

Be the spiritual warrior that you know you are. Take up your shield (psychic defense), and your weapons (your spiritual tools and spiritual contacts) and get out there onto the battlefield of life to conquer your goals. Get excited.

FORMULAE / TECHNIQUES

So we have established your familiar(s) isn't lost. However, you don't know which one(s) you have. So let's proceed to search the realms of man and spirit to locate your totem(s).

Be bold in your quest. You are taking a magickal step to be fearless and unstoppable as you move forward in creating your better life.

Now, you may already know you have one or several, so this may just be a reconnection for you. However, you may have one you didn't know about.

You may have one throughout your lifetime. You may have one or several helping you on a specific situation or project. You may have an army of helpers or one who may be temporary.

One of the keys is this: Many people want to have many familiars, as though they are gaining a coin collection. If they come to you in this way, that's great. There is a reason. However, if you are "calling in" a familiar, it is best to have one or one at a time, adding of you like, after you gain competency and a deeper connection to yours.

The level of connection is very important. The number of familiars is less important. One powerful connection is worth more than several which are not on that intense deeper level. You need that psychic link to communicate on various levels.

By the way, if you think you aren't psychic / intuitive, you are mistaken. We all are. It is a human survival instinct. I was recently a speaker at an event and this subject came up. As an example this is how to look at it: we have all had this experience or a similar one. You are walking down a busy street and you feel like someone is following you. You turn around, and surprisingly you were right. Now, that probably wasn't a threat. It was just that the person, even in a crowd, was following you longer then you subconsciously felt they should be. It was your psychic survival instinct kicking in. Just in case...

PROTECTION

These two formulae will help protect you. They work. (For a more intense one, you should get in touch with me.)

I cannot stress enough how imperative it is that you ALWAYS PROTECT YOURSELF FIRST before any psychic or spiritual work.

Prayer is one of the strongest weapons we have. We are light workers in one form or another.

1 - This is an ancient pagan spell of protection for the night when your guard is down. It is updated to Christianity by substituting angel's names for ancient deities that worked for the same intent.

This spell is also great for children to say at bedtime. It doesn't take away negativity but protects you against being harmed. Then it will leave.

You say this upon retiring for the night:

"There are four corners, on my bed,

There are four angels, at the head,

Matthew, Mark, Luke and John,

Please bless this bed that I lay on."

Amen (or So Be It)

2 - One of the Protection Prayers I formulated is to make sure you are always safe. It is meant to be used prior to any type of spiritual or psychic work:

Prayer For Power

By Rev. Maria D'Andrea

I am One with God

and let the power of God

flow in me,

through me,

and around me,

for God is ALL.

I trust the Divine Power

and all is perfect,

knowing I am always protected

and guided Divinely.

Whatever I choose

to manifest in my life

comes easily to me,

Joyfully and with perfect

harmony.

I walk the Path of White Light

in Truth, Peace,

Love,

Harmony and Health.

Thank you, Father, for I am,

You are,

WE are ONE.

Amen.

3 - Protection Stones: These can be worn or carried in a pouch (mojo bag, medicine bag) or in your pocket, purse or wallet. As long as stones, herbs or oils are within 3" of your body, they will work for you. To name a few:

You can use turquoise, apache tear, brown tiger eye, lapis lazuli or granite.

4 - Protection Herbs and Trees: Use and carry the same way as with the stones. Any part of the herb or tree will work (flower, stem, 3 petals, bark, leaf, nut, pinecone or root.) Some herbs to be utilized are - sage, tobacco, mint, broom, peppermint, aloe and carnation. Some of the trees are - willow, bamboo, oak, ash, Dragon's Blood, pine, chestnut and birch.

5 - Protection Oils: You can wear them or leave them in the room. If you wear them, you only need a drop for vibration, not for the scent - rose, wolf's bane (they now call it arnica in the stores), olive and clove.

Next: we are searching for your connection to your personal totems. It is your time for adventure.

Get your explorer hat on to go on this expedition into the unknown (safely -did you put up your protection?).

When you know what/who your totem is, you always say thank you for coming to me.

It is very important that after you recognize your familiar for what it is, you spend some time looking at the qualities it possesses. 1st - you need to see what qualities you have in common so you know who you are. If positive qualities show up, learn how to use them in the future. If negative qualities show themselves, learn how to change them to positive or to banish them within yourself. It is also a perspective. As an example: there are 2 tribes. One is attacking the other and killing everyone. This is considered negative. If on the other hand, the tribe being attacked is killing everyone who attacks, that is positive. The mindset is different. They are killing to save their lives, their families' lives and the lives of those around them. This is a spiritual outlook.

2nd - the other reason for knowing the abilities and qualities of your totem is this: you will send your totem out to help you but it has to be something your totem can accomplish because it matches its abilities. After all, if a person was great as an artist but knew nothing else, you wouldn't ask him to fix your car. Obviously that wouldn't work.

There are several techniques we can utilize. Pick one you feel comfortable with. You only need one. You may decide to try a few to see which gives you the best results. At different times, you will be pulled to different techniques. Make notes of your thoughts, feelings, senses, scents, colors, impressions if any, so you remember later. Do not try to make notes while we are on the search. Just after. Don't worry about what you'll remember. You will remember what you need to know.

SHORT PRAYER

This is a prayer from the Bible, Psalm #121. It can be utilized for all occasions, including writing it down on white paper, with black ink and keeping it in your vehicle. Or you can say it when it is called for.

"The Lord shall preserve thee from all evil:

He shall preserve thy soul"

TUNE INTO ALPHA REALITY

To gain more insight, your psychic levels are to be heightened. There are brainwaves that have been tested scientifically to show different waves for different situations. If you know (I always say we're back to knowledge) what they are, you can work with them better.

Brainwaves:

Gamma - this is your fight or flight level.

Beta - this is your normal everyday thoughts and when you communicate with others, it is on this level.

Alpha - this is your brainwave in a meditation mode and when you are functioning in a psychic / intuitive mode. My friends and students are used to me saying I'm on an Alpha high. I simply mean I'm in the psychic mode. I've had both of my sons call me at various times on the phone and after "hello," they'll ask "are you high?" My students will also do this. Now, I know what they mean, but if there are others around when they ask, others may take it differently. You can't make this stuff up...

Theta - This is a deeper level of consciousness than before. It is still on a psychic connection.

Delta - This is your deepest level. This is where someone is in a coma, where a yogi can slow his heartbeat, where psychic depths are at their lowest level.

We are working on the Alpha levels. So let's get high...

GUIDED MEDITATION

This is one form of your search. Meditation is the link between man and spirit. It vibrates to the color blue. If you'd like, you can wear or place something near you that's blue, but it isn't necessary. If you're using herbs or incense while meditating, I recommend sandalwood, bay leaves, rose, mugwort, cinnamon, or frankincense.

Never use myrrh, because it's dangerous by itself. Myrrh makes instant contact with whatever is near you on the astral plane. That gives you a 50%/50 % chance of it being negative. Frankincense brings in higher contact like angels. It can be used by itself. If you do both together, it brings quick contact with higher spiritual beings.

My suggestion is to read this into a recorder so you can listen to it without distractions. If you have to read this, it will ground you and you won't be able to meditate. It is counterproductive.

So let's travel with our minds and spirits.

First - Sit or lay down so you are comfortable and not worried about falling over. Shut off any sounds such as the phone. Preferably close shades so the light doesn't distract you.

Do NOT put music on or focus outwardly like on a candle flame.

Make sure you use your self-defense first, as always.

Closes your eyes and take 9 very slow deep breaths while focusing on your breath. Take your time but don't go so slow that it becomes uncomfortable.

With your eyes closed, move your eyes inside your lids to look about 3" above you and in front of you. Keep your focus here. This is your alpha state.

Mentally visualize yourself in a beautiful lush green forest. Look at the flowers, if any. Take your time. Be aware of the colors around you. What do you see as the landscape around you and in front of you? Is the day sunny or something else? Is it warm or cool? Are there any clouds or do you see the sun or if night then any stars or planets? Where are you?

Now, look down and see that you are on a Path. What is it made of?

As you look up, you see a bridge at a short distance in front of you where the Path leads.

You notice on the bridge, there is a fog halfway at the bridges center. You can't see the other side, but you feel safe and curious.

You decide to walk up to the bridge now. As you walk, you see what the bridge is made of and what color it is, as well as, if it has any sides or not.

You are standing at the base of the bridge now. The fog is still covering your view of the other side of the bridge. You still feel safe and curious.

You start walking onto the bridge and as you get closer to the center, you dimly see the outline of a small house. Now, you are really curious, so you walk across the bridge and stand in front of the house.

You look at the outside to see the style, the door and the door handle. You instinctively know that if you go inside you will be safe.

You turn the doorknob and enter into a beautifully lit room with round walls and a white carpet leading from you to a door on the opposite side of the room.

As you feel more, more and more comfortable and relaxed, you realize that if you ask your familiar to come to you through the other door now, you will get to meet him.

You decide this is the time and you say in a commanding voice:

Help me to listen within,

To hear, feel or know that guiding voice,

Help me to understand you better,

As my familiar,

I call you forth.

Then wait to see who comes through the door. When your familiar comes, Say: Thank You For Coming When I Call.

Spend some time letting yourself connect and being aware of how your familiar looks, moves and feel free to ask questions.

You may "hear," "see" or just "know" the answer.

By the way, you may want to ask for a name or if you don't get one, it just means that you can pick a name that you like. Important: You NEVER tell anyone its name. That is your personal link. You can say what your familiar is, what it looks like, but NOT the name.

Now, to be honest, there is an exception. We will pass down the formulae through our family for generations, at times. We only do so with family members who are working with the spiritual, psychic or the paranormal and understand. In case of an emergency, they can call on our familiar to let us know. In the case of not having any family who work with these energies (some are not open to this, which is fine. They need to walk their own Paths), much knowledge has been lost. A few in this situation have passed it down to a well-deserved initiate (student).

If you don't get a familiar at this time, it just means you should try another day or a different method. Not the same day with the same method.

When you are done, thank your familiar and say that when you want him/her to connect, at any time, day or night, he/ she will come wherever you are, in a positive way.

Next, thank it again and now you send it back through the doorway that it came in. Turn around and walk back over the bridge, along the Path to where you started.

Know that you can come back here at any time you wish to see if you have a new totem.

Take 3 slow deep breaths knowing you are coming back to your surroundings, happily and in perfect health.

Slowly open your eyes. Stretch a little where you are. Don't move and get up right away so you aren't off balance.

SACRED CIRCLE WORK

It is important for you to know you are creating sacred pace to do this work. ***But more important, is for you to realize that YOU are sacred space. Your energy becomes sacred as you work with these energies (including meditation) and when and where you work is secondary. Your aura (you) through time becomes more and more charged with positive ions/energy. When you are creating sacred space in your environment, you are heightening the energies. It's much like a battery charger.

You will need a few items for this ritual.

1 - A staff, sword, rod or any stick you find outside will do. If you have one for ritual work already, use yours if you prefer.

2 - A small white candle will do. You will need something to put the flame out with later. Never use our breath.

3 - Four clear quartz crystals of any size as long as they are around the same size.

4 - Pick one of these as an incense of your choice for purification: tobacco, frankincense, lavender or sage.

Before you start, know which way are the cardinal points- East (air), West (water), North (earth) and South (fire). These represent the directions and the 5 elements. You are the 5th element. You represent ether/spirit.

5 - Also, have everything ready. Do your self-defense always.

6 - Focus your intent on welcoming your positive familiar to you.

7 - Place the incense and the candle, matches and what you will use to snuff it out (not your breath), into the center, more or less, of where you will make your circle.

8 -Put the stones in the cardinal points in a circle, walking toward the right, clockwise. Starting in the East. You are creating sacred space. As you does this, in a commanding voice say:

I claim this as my Sacred Space. Nothing negative or harmful can get in. I declare and command that this be so. And so it is.

9 - Light the incense, and then light the candle. Next, stand in the middle of the circle, facing East.

10 - With focus, intent, expectation, patience and joy, call to your new familiar, and in a strong, sure voice, say:

By the power of three times three,

New familiar come to me.

Our connection is strong and clear,

Hear my voice, I summon thee.

Through the mist of untold time,

Come to me in Light Divine.

And as I say, so shall it be.

11 - Then wait and be aware of all your senses. You may wish to close your eyes if you see better with your third eye vision.

If you feel the urge, repeat three times - come to me.

12 - If you wish to ask questions, this is the time. Ask for a name. If you don't immediately "think" of one, "hear" it or just "know" it, then you can pick one. Remember NOBODY but you can know the name. You are creating a personal link.

13 - When you are done, you need to release it. You "called it in" so you have to "send it home". Remember to say Thank You and tell your familiar to

come whenever you call, in a positive way. Then say - "I send you forth."

14 - Next, put out the candle without blowing on it. You can put out the incense or let it run its course in the room. Pick up the crystals going in a counterclockwise direction.

15 - Put the stones into a pouch or container to be used again for the same purpose whenever you like. Place them somewhere others won't touch them.

Whenever you throw away a tool, such as the remains of a candle or incense, remember to throw it outside your home.

VISION QUESTING

This is for those who have already worked with a level of magick. Once you work with your totems, you can do this too.

Vision questing is a serious undertaking and you really need a shaman or someone with that knowledge to walk the Path with you in case you stumble. So we aren't working with this level here.

My experience when I was in my teens confirmed much of what I already experienced, since I've had these abilities from birth.

My story—

It seemed that I was preparing for my quest for years prior. In reality, it just hit me when I sought it. I was very calm since it wasn't unusual for me to see things other worldly. I "saw" the walls and the pictures on the walls of my apartment melt slowly down and disappear. In its place I saw vast darkness.

I felt safe and noticed, looking down, that I was still sitting on my couch. When I looked up again, I still saw darkness and tried to look more intensely as I looked closer. When I did, I noticed stars, planets, lights at a distance. They seemed like small dots far away and some small dots closer.

As the rest of the room started to disappear, I started to look at the solid things around me that were still not affected. As soon as I did that, I snapped back to the room as it was before, just still looking fuzzy, as though the walls were still forming back. These experiences are normal throughout my life. I sometimes wonder, what's next? (At times it can be annoying when I'm busy with other mundane things.)

Now it's your turn to do the following:

Spend a week to observe nature. Each day pick something different to focus your energy and intuitive mind on.

The first thing you do upon awakening is to tell the universe - "I am tuning in today to feel, sense, or see wherever and whatever has (the color blue. Or whatever you chose.) Then you spend your day observing. You may find you notice more blue cars then you normally do. You may have an urge to turn around and someone walking behind you has a blue shirt. Pay attention and acknowledge each situation.

You are in training.

Do this for 7 days. It doesn't matter what day you start. The important part is it really needs to be 7 for a number of reasons, some of them vibrational.

At the end of your quest, for the following 7 days, do the following:

Upon awakening, say "I want to see signs that are obvious and that I cannot misunderstand of who or what my familiar is by the end of the 7 days.

Now pay attention. You could see an advertisement with a picture of a wolf for a nearby zoo, you're changing channels on your TV and you see a wolf on a nature channel, a friend mentions he met a new friend and the last name is wolf, and so on...If it keeps coming up, you have your answer.

INEXHAUSTIBLE POWER

The spiritual plane does not have limits. It knows no boundaries. It is a vast, inexhaustible power you can tap into at will. It is everything and nothing at the same time. How great is that? It contains all you can imagine and all that you can't yet.

Let us focus now on bringing forth a new familiar from the waters surrounding our lands, various places on mother earth and flowing and contained within our bodies.

I suggest you record the following in your own voice and play it so your focus will be inward, not on outside distractions.

Sit or lay down in a comfortable position. Shut off all sounds that may be disturbing, such as the phone.

Put up your shield (protection). Close your eyes and take at least three slow breaths and as you exhale, repeat mentally the word "peace."

Think and visualize that you are on a tropical island. You are sitting at the edge of the water feeling the soft white sand under your toes; the warm breezes are swaying the palm trees near you.

You feel you are in a beautiful paradise basking in the sun. You hear the sound of distant birds as they sing their happy songs.

You wonder where your familiar might be. You gaze into the clear crystal blue water and see little fish swimming playfully. You realize your familiar is in the water happily awaiting your call in this heavenly place.

You are curious now to see your familiar. You look at the water and with serious focus, in a loud voice, you say:

My familiar hear my call,

Show yourself upon this ground,

From waters deep now come to me,

And your partner I will be.

Keep looking at the water and see what emerges. It may take a minute, but expect your familiar and it will come. It may be a mermaid, a deity, a seashell, a fish, sea serpent or seal. Don't look for anything in particular, just stay open.

Once you see your familiar, greet it and ask it for a name. If you don't get one, it's alright; you might get it the next time. Pay attention to who or what your familiar is. Size, coloring, personality and anything else you can see, hear or know. Your familiar may have a scent or may not. What are the attributes you see? Get as much detail as you can.

Ask your familiar what its main purpose or ability is. And any other questions you may think of.

Say that you have come to gain knowledge and help when needed and to reciprocate, you will send love and gratitude energy.

Then say: thank you for coming and come to me in the future whenever I call, harming none and now go forth.

Watch happily as your familiar goes back into the blue water. After all, you have a new wonderful familiar.

Relax here as long as you like. When you are ready, take 3 slow breaths and slowly open your eyes. Take your time getting up and realize that you can go back to visit at any time.

Remember, when you call your familiar, it doesn't matter now where you are or what you're doing, your familiar will come. Don't forget to send it home with thanks.

BE THE SEEKER

You are a seeker on an adventure to choose where to spend your energy to create your future.

Stay with your focus so in creating your life, you create what your intent is, not something other people say you should be or you should do. Remember, how self-fulfilling prophecy works.

You are magick in motion. You are part of all the energies in the universe. Think of it in scientific terms, as the holographic universe. If you took one cell of your body and magnified it, you would see all the information that is you. Every part of you is in that one cell. If you cut off a piece of the root of a plant, and put it in fertile soil, it will replicate the whole plant from the information in its cells. And so, with magickal work, we are unlimited. The more you work with these energies, the more in tune you will become and you will find that your abilities will automatically heighten.

So let's go on an expedition...

You are about to seek your familiar and look for a visible or audio connection. If you don't "hear" (clairaudience = clear hearing) or "see" (clairvoyance = clear seeing), be aware your familiar will still be there.

Steps to the quest:

1 - By now, you should automatically use your protection first.

2 - Allow yourself to relax, go to your alpha state by relaxing your shoulders, taking 3 slow deep breaths and putting your vision, with your eyes closed about 3" above your physical line of sight and a few inches in front of you as you breathe. You are now in your alpha, psychic sate.

3 - Mentally, think of yourself as a magi wearing a hooded robe. Notice what color you are wearing and what material it is made of. What shoes, sandals or boots are you wearing? What color and material are they made of?

The sky is just beginning to be a little darker as the sun goes down. The breeze is warm and comfortable. Now, see yourself holding in your hand a brightly lit lantern. You are the seeker of Light, Love and Truth.

You are going safely, relaxed and excitedly going into the unknown, which will now become the known.

You are on a dirt road. And as you follow the road holding your lantern high in front of you, you come to a fork in the road. You stand there a minute. You do not have to choose a direction. Simply hold your lantern of White Light high.

Visualize the living space (energy) around you and hold the lantern in front of you so whatever positive creature that is your familiar can see you and find you.

Look at the path to your right, and as a command, say:

I come to connect to my spirit familiar on the path to my right. I come harming none and call on you to come to me, doing no harm to me or my loved ones. Show yourself in a form that is pleasing to the eye and come to me now.

Then wait and see who or what comes down to path to you. Get excited. This is your direct link. Remember, your familiar is a positive connection to you and a part of you. If your familiar doesn't come right away, just repeat your command. Your familiar may be of any form. It can be angelic, animal, mythical, alien, stone, ghost, deity, elf, fairy or any other form.

Once it comes, ask for its name. If it doesn't have one, give it one. Then ask what abilities it possesses. Sometimes, you will just "know".

While your familiar stays on the right path, look over at your left path. Do the same as before feeling curious and excited. Say:

I come to connect to my spirit familiar on the path to my left. I come harming none and call on you to come to me, doing no harm to me or my loved ones. Show yourself in a form that is pleasing to the eye and come to me now.

Repeat what you did before, holding up your lantern. Wait to see what familiar comes to you. Then ask its name and again if it doesn't have one, give it a name so you can call it directly when you choose to. Then, as before, ask what abilities it possesses. You never know how you will get the information, so pay attention.

When you feel you are done, thank both of them for coming. Tell them that you will call when they are needed and now they can go forth, back to where they came until the next time.

Have them turn around and go back on the paths they came on.

Then turn around and walk back to where you started.

Put the lantern down on a flat rock near you so that you can come back at any time and it will be ready for you. It will always stay lit with the bright White Light. And you can seek other familiars the same way or come and visit the ones you already met.

4 - Relax, take 3 slow deep breaths and open our eyes. Do not try to jump up. Relax and take your time.

HOUSE PROTECTION AGAINST EVIL

It is important to know various ways to protect your home and land. You don't want to be attacked by an enemy in any form, especially when your guard is down while you are asleep.

The following is one of the formulae used in Hungary.

Ingredients:

1 - Oil of any sort, about a cup. It can be cooking oil or any other kind.

2 - Poppy seeds, about a Tablespoon will do.

3 - One chopped up garlic clove.

Remember that the measurements don't have to be exact. They were using this method since ancient times and added the right ingredients but put in the amount they felt. As an example to protect a stable, they would add a hair from the horse.

Take these ingredients and mix them well, focusing your intent on protecting your home. Hold the container where you mixed the ingredients in your hand as you say the following, standing in one place, turning to face East, toward the direction you are calling. After calling the Northern direction, face East again (to close your circle) and say the last two lines.

Say:

I call on protection from the East to shield my home,

I call on protection from the South to energies my home,

I call on protection from the West to watch over my home,

I call on protection from the North to ground my home.

No enemy can enter here. The gateway to my home and those in it is now closed.

And So Be It.

Thank the spirits of the directions for coming to you. Then take the oil mix and dipping your fingers in it, run the oil at the base of all doorways coming into your home and around all window frames.

You can save what's left of the consecrated oil for another time or just throw it away on the ground outside. It doesn't have to be ground near your home. It can be any location.

ANCIENT GUARDIAN

In ancient times, they used the birch tree as protection from negativity. So when they started to make brooms, they were made from the birch tree. Later on, they started to use the herb called "broom".

If you can get a stick or limb from the birch tree, that would be the best, but if not, then get a broom. That is made of the broom herb.

Take the stick or the broom and stand it next to your front door to block negative energy from entering. Some people still lean it across the door to block this at night.

Once in a while, use the broom to "sweep" the energy to the outside your home. It can also be used in the way you would use sage to sweep negativity out.

Also, if you're like me and like to hike, the birch makes a good staff for walking and protection—on the physical and spiritual sides. Remember, I said we are not obvious about what we're doing. It just looks like a walking stick. Although it's protection, I'm not taking it to the theatre in New York City. Might be a little obvious?

DREAM WALKING

We all dream and we can use that as a tool to a portal to find our familiars. We will open up the portal to our subconscious and gain the insight that we need.

Your subconscious mind is connected to your Higher-Self, which in turn is connected to Infinite Wisdom. We need to open the portal and see who comes in as a familiar. As always, before bed, make sure you do your self-defense. After all, even though your familiar will be positive to you, you don't want anything hitch hiking with it along the open portal.

Make sure you're in a happy mood before you lay down. You can listen to music, read a book or take a walk, anything that will make you feel positive.

Place some paper and a pen next to where you sleep.

Upon retiring, close your eyes and focus on being conscious of your body. Scan your body by placing your mind progressively on different parts of your body. If you feel any tension in that part, tell it to "relax' and when you feel more relaxed in that area, move on. Repeat this until your whole body is relaxed. When you're done, scan your body once again to make sure it's still all relaxed.

Now, take the three or more deep, slow breaths and be aware that this put you in the alpha state whether you feel so or not.

Mentally state this prior to going to sleep:

My familiar will now come to me in a way that I will recognize it. It will come in peace and let me know its name if it already has one. If not, I can name it when I'm awake. I will know its abilities or personality and how it can help me when called. I will remember my dream clearly upon awakening.

Then go to sleep.

Upon awakening, before you do anything else, write down everything that you remember. You can look at it at a later time to see the connection between your familiar and you.

If you don't get the information in the dream the first night, repeat it nightly until you do. It will come.

Sometimes you may get multiple familiars, and that's great. Just deal with it the same way. And write it in your notes.

MEDITATION - DESTRESS TO CREATE

If you're stressed, how can you create? You can't get focused or have the power for control that you need. Or for that matter, you will not have a happy expectant attitude. So, we are going to turn that around. However, there are days when we just don't feel great or are dealing with issues where we just need to take a break and put off working with your familiar.

***As a side note, on the shamanic/occult side, we deal with stress differently. Most people spend time saying they're ok and not dealing with it or putting it off. This makes it take longer to go through it. We, on the other hand, let ourselves hit bottom as fast as we can. We can spend a day or however long it takes, to dwell, cry, or yell, whatever it takes to get it out of our system. The point is: the sooner you hit bottom, the sooner you come back up.

Stress comes from numerous sources. It can be a difficult situation that you don't have any power over. It is a matter of refocusing your brain. You need to get your mind in a different space to be able to relax. Then you can refocus your energy.

As I've said, always, even if I don't constantly repeat it, do protection first. I know...you're tired of hearing it, but you will remember when you need to.

Make sure you don't have any distractions, such as a phone ringing during your meditation.

Meditation is the link between you and God. Take a few deep slow breaths, three or more. Close your eyes and focus your mind on your throat chakra (throat area).

Keep slowly breathing now. As you relax, think of what you would like to say about the situation that upset and stressed you? It doesn't have to be to anyone, it can just be you for awareness of what's really going on inside you. Or visualize the person that caused your stress and speak to them mentally. What did someone say or do to you? What did you do or say that might have triggered the situation?

Take as much time as you need. Look at every angle to gain clarity.

Now, think about the whole situation. Is there anything you can do to make it better? If the answer is no, accept it. Thank God for the positive things in your life right now. (This is an important step.) Then let go of trying to fix something you cannot fix. So your mind doesn't keep dwelling on it in a never ending circle.

If there's something you can do, decide on your course of action, and when you come out of the meditation, go and take the action and do it.

When you are ready, take a few deep breaths and slowly open your eyes.

SELF-HYPNOSIS FOR SUCCESS

This is an easy and quick technique. Since I do hypnotherapy, this technique will help you to have control over yourself, to gain your goal, to focus better and it is great for any intent you may have.

You can utilize this method in conjunction with calling in your familiar. You would do this first as a form of preparation. Then you will also be more focused and clear about what you want your familiar to help you with.

You need very few "tools" for this.

1 - All you need is a black pen or thin black magic marker.

2 - A white, non-lined 3" by 5" paper or any blank index card. The size doesn't have to be exact. We aren't that fussy.

As I said, few tools are needed for this.

Think first about what intent you are creating. Then print a short sentence or two to describe it. You may want to write it down on another paper first to get it exactly the way you'd like. Phrase it only in a positive way.

Examples: 1 - I easily and effortlessly attract the right people to gain my perfect job. 2 - I attract a love relationship that is perfect for us both. 3 - I easily say the right things comfortably when I speak to my co-workers.

Once you have it written, in print, on your index card or paper, sit in a comfortable chair that has arms. After all, you don't want to think about leaning or falling over from the chair, so it takes your focus away from what you're doing.

Make sure you don't have any noise or other distractions.

Hold the card in front of you at eye level, at a distance you're comfortable reading. Read it five times, at your own pace. Then close your eyes and drop your arm. As you drop your arm, let go of the paper. Don't think about the paper, you will let it fall wherever it goes.

Just let your mind drift. Whatever you think about, just look at your thoughts without trying to think of what you wrote or anything in particular.

Don't try to direct it. Just pay attention in a relaxed manner.

When you feel like you're done, open your eyes. Think about what your thoughts were in case it was information coming to you. Either way, you are self-programming your subconscious mind to attract, like a magnet, the intent you set for yourself.

You may want to do this once a day or whenever you feel it is right for you.

Now, you are putting out this magnetic psychic energy and your familiar will be attracted to it to help you. You may even attract friendly physical animals, like a cat or dog, near you.

SILENCE IS KEY

One of the keys to tuning in on a psychic level to your familiar is silence.

Use meditation or any other form that relaxes you. You can simply go to a place that makes you feel good. This could be a river, a stream, the ocean, mountains, trees, your room; it depends on where your connection happens to be at that moment. It does need to be a quiet place.

When you are in silence, that's when you "hear," " feel" or "sense" your psychic connection to your familiar, to yourself and to other realms.

Learn to connect inwardly. You will be amazed at how much you will grow and learn. Inner peace and awareness takes you to places you would never have known.

ANCIENT DRUMMING

In ancient cultures, as well as in modern times, the sounds of drumming and the vibrations, attract spiritual beings, including familiars.

Do I need to remind you to do your protection? You remember by now? Ok then, never mind.

The drumming sound will also have an effect on you and may put you on the psychic "alpha high."

Years ago, my friend Chief Wise Owl of the Tuscarora tribe, as a gift for helping him, spent some time recording himself drumming at various rates so I could use his sounds. It was a very private and generous thing for him to do. Being that he had a sense of humor, as shamans tend to do with each other, on the tape, he labeled it as "Chief Drumming."

It doesn't matter what style or size the drum is. They all have their own sound. Preferably you want a deeper sound for big familiars - bear, guardians, horses and so on. You would use a lighter sound for smaller familiars. If you don't have the two main sounds, don't worry about it. They all work.

Make sure you are calm and in a positive, focused mood. Start your drumming by matching the rhythm of your heart. You can take your pulse to see what your pace is at the time.

Keep drumming until a familiar comes to you. In whatever form it comes in or what realm (physical or spiritual) it comes from, it is here for you. You called it in. Keep drumming while you ask its name, abilities, purpose and if it will work with you.

When you are finished, thank it for coming and let it know you might call on it again at some point. You don't need to say when because you don't know and because there isn't a sense of time with them.

If you don't have a familiar come, it just means to do it again at another time. You did it correctly. Good job.

SCRYING FOR YOUR FAMILIAR

Witchcraft, which is a positive nature belief system, uses this technique frequently, as do other masters.

Do not confuse scrying with skrying. Scrying is what you will be able to do to find a familiar. Skrying is out-of-body travel to the etheric side.

Scrying is a very ancient method to acquire information, direction and you can use it to help you to find your familiar. It means "seeing" psychically clear pictures or visions. This is done on shiny surfaces that can have a reflection.

Remember, this is a tool from ancient times. So the surface can be clear water, a piece of quartz crystal or crystal ball (which can be clear or black for best results), a mirror (some of us noticed that in Snow White, the mirror was for scrying – getting information. It's funny when you look at some stories and situations in life in general from our perspective), steel that's polished (we've used swords and knives) and cups or bowls that either have been painted in shiny black paint at the bottom or hold enough water to have a reflection (the bottom must have a solid color not to distract your gaze, black or white is good).

This form of divination helps you to focus and heightens your psychic perceptions. Use it judiciously.

You will need a scrying tool. Any shiny surface that reflects clearly as mentioned will do. You don't need to get a crystal ball. Unless, of course, you find this method resonates to you and might want one as a choice.

Story—

When I was in my teens, my gaze went to the bubbles in a bubble bath. It captivated me and I started to see images, I didn't want to look away. Mainly out of curiosity. As I stared, I saw "Aunt Nanny," as she was called, outside her house, sweeping, which she was known to do.

Then the scene shifted and I just knew it was showing a time down the road, and I saw how she was going to pass on. At the time, it of course upset me. So I told someone in her family, who knew I was psychic. And a month or two later, that's what occurred. Now, it would've been preventable if she listened and was more careful but you know how it is with free will. It did make it easier for some of her family, in that it wasn't as much of a shock and her family really tried to connect more to her.

So at times, it will trigger automatically. At other times, we do so consciously.

First, you know what I'm going to say, right? Use protection. Shield up.

Put yourself in a psychic, alpha state of mind. You can use the slow breathing method.

Let's use a scrying bowl for now. Make sure it is washed and clean. You can fill it about ¾ of the way with water ahead of time.

Put it so you could have light at an angle toward it, which could be sunlight, candle light, or whatever is the light of your choice. You don't want direct light, because it will disturb your vision.

Stare into the bowl. Look into it with a neutral attitude. Don't look for anything specific. Let it flow to you. Keep staring until you start seeing images in it.

Verbally chant 3 times:

By break of dawn,

By starlit night,

My familiar comes to me tonight.

Come show yourself,

Connect to me,

Let me "see,"

So mote it be.

*** Important- Do not try to stay focused. After a while your vision can become fuzzy, blurry and unfocused. This is what you want. This vision is psychic. If you refocus, you are focusing on the physical plane and won't be able to see with your third eye psychically. The Key is being unfocused.

It's sometimes like watching TV. You may "see" scenes, people, animals, whatever you need to now, in color or black and white. One isn't better then another. The point is the information.

Once you are finished, think about what you just saw. If you didn't see your familiar, try again the next day/night until you do.

Get up and throw the water away outside your home. Then you can rinse out the scrying bowl and put it away for another time, or put it back in the kitchen. We are very flexible. In tribal times, many still needed the bowl for food, while others kept it separately to keep the energy heightened in the same "tool" every time it was used.

By the way, crystals come in various sizes. It doesn't make a difference in scrying. The only way to pick one is to see which you have a pull toward.

You are a spiritual warrior of light. You are entering a different realm, the extra-dimensional universe and beyond.

CHAPTER FIVE
DISCOVER HOW TO WORK WITH YOUR MAGICKAL SIDE

In the game of life, you need to know how to play to win. Like chess, you need to know all the information before you can make your move. So let's gain the knowledge you need.

A familiar will come to you on its own when needed or you can "call one in". At times, they will just pop up, without a reason. You are not always aware of their assistance, but that doesn't mean you aren't receiving support. Now, you can consciously work with yours.

Always do your protection, but also have fun with it. This is exciting. You are about to go on a journey with your familiar. If you have several, only work with one at a time in the beginning. Your focus will be important. You are unlimited in how you can improve your life.

Being able to control the direction of your life gives you power that others don't have and probably aren't aware of. So use it consciously to elevate yourself.

You have been working throughout my book to change your perspective and to see things in a different way than most of society. You can create new goals and be able to align with your familiars.

It always strikes me in a funny way that people think that magickal beings are around us or that they are helping us, yet they don't connect it as WE are also magickal beings. You truly have to love the humor of the universe. Come on, you know it's funny.

When we focus on a goal, we do what is necessary to bring it in on the spiritual and the physical sides of reality. We work on both planes of existence. But once we've initiated all we can, we let it go. We call it a self-forgetting state of mind. There are altered states of consciousness that we can tap into. When you are in the self-forgetting phase, you let go of your control. You give it up to the Universal Mind/God or whatever name you resonate with. This is an important step. I know, it's hard to give up your control, but you know you are not creating all by yourself. You have Divine Power, your familiars and you work it on the physical side also. You have to find your peace within yourself to trust and "know" that whatever your intent, it is coming to you. It's on its way.

Through working with the occult, you'll learn to trust it without question.

Whenever you are creating your intent, you will have dedication to doing it right and you don't question the outcome. Just expect it. When I'm doing a reading for a client who's working occult for a goal, I don't check to see if the outcome of what my client is working on will "hit," because that will delay or cancel it.

Think of it this way: if you have a friend going to the store later during the day and you ask her to pick something up for you while she's there, she will say yes. You will automatically say thanks because you know you'll get the item even before she bought it. So we say thanks to familiars at the time we work with them because we know the outcome in the same way. However, if you call your friend every two minutes while she's on the way, you will slow her down or she's going to think that you don't trust her word that she's going to get your item and decide in that case, why should she? So you either slowed her down or cancelled everything. It takes time or an experience that sets it into motion to develop that trust, that "knowing," but it will come. Wait for it...wait for it...there it is!

Trust in the process. It has worked for centuries, why wouldn't it work now?

You are discovering a wellspring of knowledge and spiritual growth. Use it constructively.

Some of us do out of body travel. I wrote an article once and called it *"How to Travel Without Luggage."* I did say we look at things differently...You really need a sense of humor...right?

Going to the astral realms consciously, changes our perspective on life. Think of the astronauts, having a different perspective when they're in outer space looking down on the planet. Even flying on a plane and looking down at the clouds gives you a different viewpoint. You can't come back from those experiences and look at the world the same way. You are also embarking on a journey now with your familiars that will change your perspective on life.

To understand some of your own power, look at it this way: most people look at your body as containing your spirit, your soul. I've found the reverse. When you look at your aura, your energy body, you see colors and other objects emanating from your physical body. It permeates through you and around you. It is larger than your body. This is YOU. This is your spirit, your soul. The body is contained within it. So when we do spiritual protection, we focus around the outside of the aura (you), not just around your body. That won't work past a point because you're leaving yourself partly open. How amazing are you?

There was Hun eagle archers, as it is passed down, that aimed at the sky. Knowing with Zen energy, they would hit their targets, wherever the targets were. Sometimes you have to aim high (spiritually) to hit a target on the ground (physical plane).

Go back to when you were a child and you looked for new challenges, new things to explore and try. You were curious, excited, happy and/or playful as you learned. This is how you want to be. Get your shoes on and head toward your new adventure. Yay. Exploration into the unknown with your familiar beside you to guide you and help you get to your destination is exciting.

What we do is very serious, but that doesn't mean we are. After all, knowing you can co-create gives you a different perspective on everything. Envision the possibilities.

Expand your view of reality, your consciousness. You are creating it. We live in a multi-dimensional universe. Shaman, witches and others on the spiritual path have traveled these places for centuries. Now, it's your turn to understand and incorporate your knowledge into your life.

You are at a point where the paranormal is now normal. (Remember the glasses example.)

You now know that you are expanding your consciousness to be broader and include all forms of energy to work with. Including those seen and unseen, humanity, animals, deities, elves, things that fly, swim, run and go bump in the night.

You are connected to the mystical, psychic and physical realms. It is as though you now have a private phone line to the Divine. All is energy and you are going to work with your familiars to form your objectives. Of course, we only do positive, never harming others. I know I say that a lot. I do that so if anything like an obstacle comes up in your life, you will automatically handle it in a positive way. Look at how aware you are already.

Success is saying yes, before you're ready. Jump into the stream of never-ending energy. Ride that wave.

Let your intuitive, your psychic side guide you. Let it inspire you. Inspire = in spirit. It is within you already. Just pay attention consciously. God gives you the ability to manifest.

You have superpowers. I know you don't need a cape, but then, who knows?

On to the "How To" part.

Now that you are connected to your familiar, pick a small goal before you start. You want to start off with something easy.

To put you into the right frame of mind to connect, think of something positive and put yourself in a happy mood. After all, you are on an adventure. Cosmic Law states that like attracts like. Later on, when you've already worked together, you'll notice you'll be serious about what you're doing and happy at the same time while calling your totem to you.

Look to see which qualities of your totem are compatible with you. Also realize that you may not have that "pull," that affinity with a totem, but may need its abilities for whatever intent you are working on. That's perfectly fine. You can still work together. Remember, it may be temporary for only that intent. Don't limit yourself.

7 STEPS TO VICTORY

Step 1 - Go to a place where you won't be disturbed. Shut off anything that makes noise like the phone. You don't want distractions. You can be outside or inside. It is a preference or convenience at the time. Some people go to the same place continuously. You can do so, but it isn't necessary when dealing with familiars.

Step 2 - Make sure you are very clear about your intent and about which familiar you will be calling in.

Step 3 - Even if I forget to mention it, don't forget to ALWAYS use the psychic self-defense. Even though you're calling a positive totem, you are opening a doorway to another realm. In doing so, you want to make sure you don't get a negative hitch-hiker sneaking in.

Step 4 - Put yourself in the intuitive, psychic mode, also known as the alpha state of mind. (I really just say it's an alpha high, because that's what it feels like.) You can take deep, slow breaths, remembering to drop your shoulders and relaxing. You need at least three or it won't work, but you can do more. Go by what you feel. As you do so, you can close your eyes and look up about 3" and a little in front of you to connect quicker.

Step 5 - Now you're ready. Call your familiar to you in a commanding voice. You are the one in control of the situation. You may be partners of sorts, but you are still in command because you're on the physical plane. Say:

I now call forth (say the name you gave to your familiars) to come to me. Come in a positive way, and cause no harm.

Then stay still and wait. You will have a "knowing" feeling or a sensation that you are not alone. If you don't feel that, just repeat it three times. At that point, it will be automatically with you.

Remember, your totem can be any being, in any realm, including animate and inanimate objects like gemstones or various parts of nature.

If you are calling in a familiar that is new to you, for this one intent, you will not have named it. Then you can say:

I now call forth the master of the highest order for the purpose of - (state your purpose clearly) to come to me. Come in a positive way, and cause no harm.

Step 6 - Give it a minute and clearly say:

Bring this outcome swift and strong in a way that I like. Do this in a positive way until it is done. Do not stray form my intent for you and I are now connected. I am, you are, we are of one purpose. So Be It.

Step 7 - Thankfulness is important to keep the balance. Your familiar will help you and in return your "payment" is giving thanks. So say:

Thank you for answering my call. Complete this task and now go forth.

After you call in a familiar, you have to send it out to work on the intent. It cannot leave until you do so. You brought it in, now you send it out or home. This is a very important step. If for some reason you forgot, do so whenever you remember because it will stay with you until you do. Do not forget. . .

MEDICINE BAGS

There are several names for medicine bags, such as mojo bags, spell pouch and more. They are all bags that you can buy or sew that keep your spiritual "tools" or medicine. You can wear them, carry them, place them in a special place or place them on an altar.

The color of the bag represents your intent. If you are not sure which to use, then pick white. That keeps it positive.

All colors have a vibrational frequency, as proven by science. This is a great thing. I love when we've been doing things for centuries and now science can prove it. Funny universe.

Some Color meanings of pouches:

Red - strength, love

White - keeps things positive, all-purpose, enhancer, purity, awakening

Black - power, will power, control (you'd use it as control over yourself and your abilities)

Blue - trust, calm, peace, connection to other realms

Orange - prosperity, sexual energy

Purple - strength, Higher Powers

Yellow - happiness

Gold - attaining

Pink - healing, universal love

Green - love, healing, finance

Pick a color for your pouch that works with your intent.

Place something inside your bag that represents your familiar. This can be a small statue, a small horseshoe or four leaf clover, a picture, a sigil, a feather, a sea shell; some shaman will also use a bone (that would be part of the animal they're connected to). It doesn't matter what it is. What matters is that it represents your totem to you.

This is called Sympathetic Magick. The Law, like attracts like is at work here. As an example, some people who understand this might wear gold jewelry because that means wealth (or money) to them. When they wear it, it is like a magnet attracting more gold (money).

When you place something in the pouch to represent your familiar, it will hold some of your familiars' energy and you will have a connection to your totem whenever you wear or carry the pouch.

Next, if you're working on a particular intent, place something that represents your intent in the pouch also. Leave it in the pouch until your purpose is achieved.

Once your goal is met, take the item representing your intent and bury it anywhere outside your home.

Do NOT bury your familiar (He won't like it and it's a level of disrespect, disconnect and basically you're ending your link.) If you are done working with this particular totem, you can say thank you and you are sending him/ her forth. Then take the item out of the pouch and either put it somewhere safe for another time or place it outside in the woods (park, yard, etc.). Depending on who your familiar was, it may call for taking it and putting it in a lake, ocean, stream, waterfall... I could've just said water, but it wouldn't give you the same mental pictures. After all, what we do is serious, but we're not. So which body of water resonated with you?

MAGICK, MAGICK EVERYWHERE

By now, you are getting the hang of the magickal worlds.

You are unlocking the power within you.

You can conjure your familiars and create, create, create. What a wonderful world.

Understanding the Laws of nature allows us to improve our lives, if we so choose. We are the magi who co-create. We are one with the various realms and are always on the path of learning. We are seekers and we are teachers of the art and science of these worlds.

We are by no means better than others; we are simply different, on a different Path and enlightenment. You cannot work with energies and various beings without the knowledge to do so safely.

There are numerous forms that you can utilize and some of them are in this book. You must choose which form resonates with you. It won't always be the same form due to different situations and depending on where you are at that point in your life.

There is spell crafting, sigils, ceremonies, divination, prophecy, ministry in whatever form your belief system has, rituals and much more.

Here we are placing our focus on familiars so you can work magick right away. It takes years of study to come up with quick plans, so I tend to laugh at the word - quick. But as long as it works as it does, that's all that matters so we're good to go.

The astral plane is really where we do our work. Think of it this way so you are conscious of what happens. After all, you don't get to drive the car without the key.

I coined the phrase years ago teaching to make it easily understood, that I call "TAP" ©. Think of a triangle. At the bottom left point is *Thought*. This is where we decide what we are manifesting, what our intent/goals are. At the top point is the *Astral*. This is where everything happens and forms. Then on the right bottom point of the triangle is the *Physical plane*. This is where it becomes form on the physical plane.

So...TAP— you put it out in *Thought*, it forms on the *Astral plane* and comes down to the *Physical plane* so you have what you were focused on.

When you get to the point in your life where you are more self-aware and aware of how everything really works, you sometimes get fall out. This means that for a short time you might feel you don't really fit society. And you don't. Most of society is asleep, for lack of a better word. Some are in the process of awakening. YAY. And then there is you. Once you know how and why you can create, there's no going back to unawareness. You opened the box already, but isn't it a great surprise how much you are capable of doing now? The feeling that you're alone or that you don't fit will tone down. After all, if you have a direct link to the universe, to Divine Power, and those of us already on this Path of Light, you will realize you're not alone. You have connections now on both sides of reality. Woohoo, yay, let's go manifest something...

Go ahead and pick a goal. Be serious about what you want to manifest.

High magick and your awareness will transcend the mundane and you will see, hear and know things that others don't.

There are numerous systems in all cultures to help elevate you to this level, such as yoga, meditation, Taoism and much more.

Your training with me focuses your intuition, your psychic abilities to a level of mastery. Make sure you move on your first instinct. Take responsibility for your thoughts and actions. If you don't like where you are in life, that's ok, now is the time to change it.

Don't make the mistake of creating by putting off decisions, not taking action or not setting goals. (Goals can be small like going for a walk.) When you don't think about things and just go day to day, you are making a decision inadvertently. Create on purpose with conscious choices. Use your imagination.

Don't think you aren't at your goal yet. Think about how you will be when you reach it. Be self - motivated. Although a cheering section is great to have. This brings us to the people in your life.

It is very important to stay away from negativity as much as possible. If you have family and friends who get excited about your achievements, they will be giving you not only support but giving you the momentum to keep achieving more and more.

If you have people who are neutral or not thrilled for your successes, stay away from them because they will drain your energy (they are known as psychic vampires) and slow you down or even cancel you out. You know we can't have that.

I've noticed that when you are fearful or feel guilty, you stop the flow and sometimes even reverse it.

Prosperity is our given right. Don't reject what God is giving you; allow it in with an open heart.

As an example, some people feel guilty about having too much money or feel they shouldn't have it for other reasons in the first place. This is a very big mistake. Many Christians misunderstand what the Bible says. It never says money is evil, it basically says you need to put God first before money. Pagans and other belief systems don't have that outlook. First, money is just energy in motion. Think of the barter system. Second, if you are starving in the street, who are you going to help? You have to do well, so you can help others.

If you still feel bad or guilty, when you have a lot of money, pay your bills, buy what you want, take care of your family and if you have an overflow then help others.

It's also funny how when you release the fear and just have fun, the happier you are the more money you attract, the more money you attract, the more fun. It is fun when you aren't worried because you "know" it's coming in, you will have no doubt, no doubt...and it's fun to help others. It makes us feel good. It is a circle.

Another important part is to put back and to help others from the heart. It doesn't always mean money.

If you give someone helpful advice, give them a ride to work, help with emotional support, it's putting back. You don't have to analyze, just do things for others when situations come up.

Think big. Don't limit yourself. Divine Power didn't, why should you? God made you with many abilities. You are versatile. You have untapped power that you can tap into now. That's why some of my books are a series called *"Yes You Can."* I believe in you. I truly know you can get to your goals. You are meant to be a winner in life, so let that winning streak in.

We are calling in familiars so you don't have to do things alone. They want to help. Let them. You can master any familiar, including a wild animal, physical or etheric. You have those traits within you. Go and be wild.

We are never ordinary people. We all have something about us that makes us unique. So go and be your unique self.

At times people get upset because they feel we are holding back some information when they ask questions. No we aren't, but some things you can't explain because they're not yet ready to understand it. But we try. It's like being in college and explaining to someone in grade school all the technical knowledge you have, expecting them to understand. Another reason is that there are no words in languages for what we see. If you see a color on the astral plane that doesn't exist on ours, how can you describe it? We do try

And so we have what we call Mystery Schools.

This is why I say to breathe slowly, and focus differently with your inner eyes. When you are breathing deeply and slowly, your muscles relax, making it easier to let go of the outward focus on the physical and go to your inner power. There's always a method to my madness. OK, maybe not madness, but there is always a reason for my methods.

TOTEM PLUS YOU = SUCCESS

Your familiars will be of immense help in gaining your goals. It is a matter of connecting as a friend, not just when you need help. You are going to build together and have fun together.

Before you start, you need to be very clear about your goal. How are you picturing your success? If you are not sure of your direction, how do you think your familiar can assist you? If there's no clear direction, then there's nowhere to go. You need an astral pathway. So let's build one.

Once you have your goal, you will need 2 items.

1- Something that represents your goal. Is it a beautiful home? Is it a particular fast car? Or (fill in your personal goal). It can be a picture of the style of the home you'd like or a small toy car like the one you want.

2- Now get something small that represents the totem that will assist you.

3- You will put these 2 items somewhere that you will see them every day. This could be by your bedside, placed in a drawer you open every day or anywhere you feel you can't miss them.

You are building an energy stream, a link that connects you to your goal and your familiar.

Let's try a money spell, just for practice.

Take some folding money (or if you have a gold coin to represent wealth) and place it on your altar, table, dresser or anything with a flat surface to represent your altar for now. Light a white or green candle placed next to it.

Heighten your psychic energy by taking deep quick breaths seven times. (seven is a spiritual number.) Call in your familiar and state what your goal is and that you are summoning your familiar for help in this venture. Take the money and hold it in your hand. Feel its texture, notice its scent, is it old or new, rub it, touch it, play with it a moment. Relate to it physically. We are creating in the physical plane.

Light your candle. Focus on the money. What will you do when you have it? Talk to your familiar verbally about why you are creating it and appreciating the help. Think of the people you can help. Say how much you like/love money. It's only energy. If you can't like it, why would it come? Like attracts like. If you don't love/like it, it won't come.

Focus your thoughts and repeat three times:

Money and I are one. It comes to me easily, effortlessly and in a way that I like. I AM a money magnet.

In a loud voice, state:

NOW!

Immediately put out the candle. Never blow it out, use anything else such as a snuffer, aluminum foil, etc.

Tell your totem to go forth, harming none, and bring the money to you.

Throw the candle away outside your home. You are setting it free to go work for you.

THE OPEN DOOR

Decide on your intent. Then look to see which deity, apparition, ghost, nature spirit or any other ethereal being has the qualities that will help you in moving ahead toward gaining abundance in your life.

You are going to open a doorway to your abundance, so it can just come to you. You are letting it flow to you. You are not going to work hard on it; you are going to accept it as your spiritual right.

Allow the universe to do its job and give you what you are focused on.

The important concept to remember is that you are not working hard to get to your goal. You are relaxing, putting out what you are to manifest with trust and ease because you are a magnet to attract it to you.

Follow these steps:

1 - Do your protection and shield up.

2 - Enter into your alpha, psychic mode by taking at least three slow deep breaths keeping your eyes closed and focusing about 3" above your physical line of sight and a little in front of you.   This

automatically puts you in that mode, whether you feel it or not.

3 - Visualize a place that makes you feel good. It can be a forest, lake or a city. Whatever resonates with you.

Take your time and look around comfortably. Feel a soft warm breeze blowing around you lifting up your mood even more. See birds swiftly flying overhead and the sun drenching you in its golden rays.

4 - Now you call the totem you picked to come to you. Call for the Master of the Highest Order for all (angels or apparitions or spirits or whatever ethereal being you picked prior to starting) to come to you, in a positive way now. Then wait a minute. Say you are welcoming the Master to walk with you on your journey for abundance and you are happy to have a traveling companion.

5 - As you look around, you see a locked door. You walk up to it and stop in front of it, wondering why it has a lock hanging from its door handle. As you think of this question, you intuitively know it is because you can't get in if you are resisting having prosperity from fear or past experience and so pushing your abundance away from you. Take a minute and ask yourself, are you ready for abundance and prosperity? Do you trust that the universe wants you to be happy and without hardship? Of course you're ready. That's why you found this book and me. You are blessed with the unlimited energies of the cosmos. Get excited. You are about to become the master of your life. Your soul yearns for happiness.

Look at the door and what it is made of. Look at the lock and notice how big it is. When you look down over to your right, next to the door frame, you notice an orange rock. You go over to it instinctively and pick it up. As you do so, underneath it, you see the key to the lock on the ground. Pick it up and walk to the lock. Put the key in and open the lock.

Now, at this time, you realize that the size of the lock was the size of your resistance. Since you opened the lock, you've let go resisting your life being better and happier.

6 - Look to your left and you will see a shiny golden bucket. Pick it up and you will carry it inside with you.

7 -Open the door and walk inside with the familiar you called in, at your side. You will see a gigantic Hall of Lights that seems to never end. Everywhere you look; there is unending abundance in various forms.

There is an area with money, gold, copper, silver, gemstones of all different bright shinny colors, all forms that represent money and financial wealth. You look in a different section and notice very, very old people running around, exercising and being active in general as if very young. This is your health and regenerating area. As you keep looking, you notice a different area with families enjoying each other, friends laughing together, lovers embracing each other and so on. This is your relationship area.

Take your time and look at the different areas of abundance.

8 - Now, tell your familiar to walk over to the first area that you need to increase the most in your life right now and that you will follow. Let your familiar go at whatever pace it chooses and follow. What is it representing? Take your time and look at what or who is in that space and decide you are happy to accept abundance from there. (If you are hesitant and not ready yet, that's alright, you can come back at any time you wish to collect your abundance.) Look for something small to take back with you that represents this area. Place it in your bucket.

Tell your familiar if there is anywhere else to go at this time, you will follow. When your totem starts to move, follow and go through the same process. Keep adding to your bucket.

When your familiar is done for now, say that you are both leaving for now and both of you go back to the door where you started.

9 - Walk back outside; place the bucket on the ground near the door so you can use it again, if you choose to come back. Take out the small representations and put them in your pocket. You are bringing them back with you on the ethereal plane.

10 - Place the key under the orange stone again, but do NOT put the lock back on the door. You are now open to abundance and no longer need to limit yourself and lock yourself out of limitless abundance.

11 - Thank your totem for coming with you and being your guide on this journey. And that you may call again if you come back here at another time.

12 - Take a few quick breaths and focus on the physical location you are in and open your eyes slowly.

13 - Take some time and think of all that happened. Whenever you are working on a particular focus (wealth, love, etc.), visualize the small item you brought back with you (which is now contained on the etheric side connected to your aura) and "know" it is coming to you, so you can just relax and expect it. Put physical effort in, but don't frustrate yourself because you know it's already on the way. If you get frustrated, visualize the small item that relates to the situation.

Leave all your options open, you don't know where your abundance will come from, but you do know it is coming.

You are a magnet for abundance.

WE DO NOT FIT SOCIETY

I know that's not your usual advice, but then it's me...

We don't try to fit society. We honor the laws, of course, but we think out of the box. And there is a reason why.

If we all thought the same way and tried to always do what everybody else does, what would happen to creativity? It would be a sad, boring world. And the world would get stagnant. There wouldn't be any growth. Society wouldn't have trains, planes or automobiles. I don't know about you, but I like those things.

Creative energy doesn't just limit us to the artists. It includes inventors, free thinkers and many more interesting types of people.

To achieve, you have to either try something different or in a new way. My mother was a writer, among other things and saw things in a creative way. At the same time, one of the things my father always said (he was an inventor, among other things) was to look at the world in a different way than others. Look from another direction and you will see unbelievable things and get new ideas or new ideas for old ways. So be open.

Even if you're basically analytical, which you need for balance, you have some creative aspects, if you're reading my book. Use the tools God gave you, whatever they may be.

You will know which rules, ideas to follow and when to go on your own path. Use your judgment, ethics and heart. Genius doesn't come from complacency and always being like everyone else. Trust your instincts.

You are the master of your life. Be conscious making decisions, even small ones that affect you. If you love the sun and warmth, will you be thrilled going on vacation in the arctic? If you love the cold, what possessed you to decide on the Amazon on vacation?

Each decision creates a ripple in the stream of life. Flow in the direction that makes you happy and leads you toward your goals.

CHAPTER SIX
UNLOCK THE SECRET CODE OF FAMILIARS

Remember that each animal or other form of totem has its own abilities and knowledge for you to gain from and work with.

If you are drawn to a particular totem, it means there's a connection. You may decide to work with it. At times this can turn into a long term connection. Or it could just be for a specific time or situation.

Here you will find their basic traits, so you're off to a good start. If there is a particular familiar that you have a pull toward, you can look into its traits more.

You can find these traits through meditation, asking for the information before you go to sleep and ask that the information is clear and understandable to you. If you are looking a trait up through a book, as an example, look for the real physical animal traits.

Be bold. Be daring. Be you. Be aware of your connections and consciously work with them. Don't let this time go by when you could be moving forward in your life and gaining romance, finance, basically abundance in whatever area you choose. It is your Path, so it is your decision.

You've already read what you need to do; now it's the part where you work with totems and start enjoying your life more.

The ideas and formulae revealed in this book work, but only if you are willing to look at the spiritual world in a different way. We see things differently than most of society and that is a good thing.

When you think of Einstein, Tesla, Bell, Da Vinci and many others, you realize that none of them looked at the world the way society did. Otherwise we may not have a phone, as an example. Be innovative and be an explorer of the universe and all its possibilities. Are you packed and ready for the exploration?

You can conquer your obstacles and fears and start toward the joyful areas of your life. Don't tell others what your goal is unless they are supportive. You don't want them to cancel you out or slow you down. You can tell them after you've reached your goals...You need to ignore negativity that you hear from radio, TV and any other source. When you look you will find every day has some happiness. Even if it's just that the sun was out. Train your mind to look for the positive.

You need a positive, unflinching, spiritual warrior attitude to work with your familiars.

Allow yourself to go for your intent, your dreams. They can become a reality and you're not alone. Your familiars are there to help you every step of the way.

Working with your familiars will change your outlook on the world. They will help you create exactly what your intent is focused on.

Once you gain the first goal, you can take it to the next level and pick another one that moves you up and up, and so forth. In the beginning, I suggest an easy goal that will give you a quick confirmation of how it works. This will tell your subconscious mind that you've manifested it (with some positive help) already and to expect the next one to work as well. At the same time, you're telling the universe that you are serious about achieving your goals and the universe will say ok, there's someone listening and working on things so I'm sending you the next outcome. You have to love the workings of the universe...

Time is of the essence. Why would you wait to be happier? Let's start taking action on it now. You will be very impressed with yourself.

Keep your thoughts optimistic. Be a pioneer, use your imagination and explore new ways to move your life to higher and higher goals. Be confident because you no longer walk alone. With your familiar(s) at your side, you have untapped, as of yet, talents and abilities at your beck and call.

I'm always intrigued by how people are moving up in the world once they can manifest. It just makes me feel good.

I'm passing on this knowledge because, on a selfish level, the better you do, the better the world gets and that has direct impact on me (and others). It's the domino effect. If I can be of further help in your learning in any of my fields, you know where to find me. This is who I am. I'm not writing this and disappearing when you need to ask something about this book (or my other books). As much as I kid around, I'm serious about making your life better.

Over her lifetime and as a Spiritual Leader, Maria D' Andrea has provided excellent psychic guidance and enlightenment to many people, assisting them on their own personal path of spiritual self discovery.

THE HORSE

This includes all animals related to the horse (Pegasus, unicorn, donkey, zebra, mule and burro). A horse will bond easily with us.

These animals radiate strength, power and are protective. One of the traits we notice is how the horse has a way of knowing how someone else relates to him/her. If you ride, you will know that the horse knows right away who's in charge. If you don't know what you're doing, the horse will take over and go in the direction he/she decides on. If the horse doesn't like what's going on, he/she will simply run off, sometimes just for a short while to gain balance. The horse at times has an ardent desire just to run.

Walking, movement of any type, going distances is natural and refreshing. Some are loners while other horses are more social.

They are comfortable with hard work, knowing the results will come.

Utilized as transportation, they will take you on a journey within yourself and show you your inner self. They will take you to where you need to be in your life.

They will take care of you, but you also have to take care of them. To be nurturing to them. It goes both ways. Which means you can be nurturing or /and like being nurtured.

Pegasus is the winged horse in mythology, which ascended to heaven after his birth. Pegasus represents wisdom, fame and a warrior in the air and on land. In the occult field, Pegasus connects to the east, which connects to the element of air, wisdom and intellect. Of course, he can also take you on a fun flight of fancy.

Horse energy speaks of the ability to do work in both realities. How can you use these abilities?

Story—

My son, Rick has always had his Pegasus as one of his familiars. Years ago, he had a chain with a Pegasus pendant to help him connect faster to his familiar. Rick charged the pendant for protection, among other things. He was working at the Renaissance Festival in upstate New York doing Readings.

He was speaking to a girl who told him of her problems and that she was scared. Rick told her not to worry and said he would send Pegasus to take care of her. He then lent her his pendant.

She called Rick later and said she was holding the pendant and felt Pegasus nuzzle her and she tried psychically to put a noose around him. He didn't let her and flew away.

But since Pegasus was part of Rick, she was actually (unknowing) trying to control Rick and his subconscious wouldn't let that happen.

You have to admit, it's funny how it works

At another time, he was still new to familiars. So, this is his other...

Story –

Rick had a Pegasus always coming to him. He was speaking to his friend, Mark about this. (Rick just called as I'm writing his story. You have to love synchronicity.) To get back to it...Mark said to picture Pegasus. So he did this. Then he said to picture sitting on Pegasus, which Rick did. The next step was to picture being in (into) him, which he did.

When he did this, Rick found himself on a flight. Great experiences.

THE SNAKE

This also connects to any form of the snake, such as a lizard, etc. When you watch a sea serpent or a snake, you'll notice it moves in various directions instead of directly forward. It has a direction it's moving toward, but may make an indirect path to it. You may have a goal but may need to take various steps to get there.

Snakes were used with venom medicine to heal; on the other hand, they can also be poisonous. My friend, Chief Wise Owl, used snake venom for healing, but obviously you need to be an expert with it to utilize it correctly. That can also include using poisonous words that hurt others.

A snake is connected to energy rising (Kundalini) toward the heavens as it uncoils. To us that means enlightenment and the ability to rise above the mundane. It connects us to the source of ancient wisdom.

They are connected to romantic relationships and infinity. The snake has the ability to hold her own tail and become an infinite circle or hold someone else's to create a never ending circle with them.

This also represents transformation and changes as it can shed its skin and renew. It will help you in these endeavors.

THE SQUIRREL

The squirrel family includes chipmunks, woodchucks, prairie dog, and so on.

Although some are loners, others are more community minded. They can hesitant at times to trust. Squirrels will usually run away from you, until they know you. Even then they can be a little distant.

They have extensive communication with others of their kind. Therefore, communication is a natural skill. (Hint, hint.) This can make you a smooth talker and you can use it in a positive manner to achieve goals.

Squirrels are organizers, generous (they help each other), good providers and have the ability to be a survivor. After all, they store food away for the winter. They know when to run away and when to attack (protecting their young, as an example). Do you find yourself drawn to them?

Story –

My son, Rob has a squirrel as one of his familiars. Even when he was young he related to them. And they related to him.

Most people tell their children to stay away from squirrels because they bite (it's our protective instinct). However, they usually run away from us if we get too close.

I noticed that when Rob would go outside, one would start to follow him, then another came, and another, and so on. Pretty soon it looked like he was the Pied Piper. The funny part was that he wouldn't really pay attention because he was used to it. And he just took it for granted.

One day I noticed he was taking some food outside and asked why. He simply said he has a particular squirrel that comes for food each day. When I looked outside, there he was, sitting on a step of the house and feeding the squirrel out of his hand. Then another one came to be fed a few steps away.

I noticed the next day that the squirrel would come and sit on the step and wait until Rob went outside. And he still has that connection to squirrels, among other familiars.

Another familiar Story –

When Rob was little (pre-kindergarten), a friend of mine, Robin, gave him a baby duck for Easter. We were in a small apartment at the time, so the main happy person was Rob. You could tell there was an immediate spiritual connection because of how they both reacted.

Normally, children would think it's cute but the novelty would soon wear off. But that didn't happen. The minute the baby duck was put on the floor, the baby duck went straight to Rob (and there were other people in the room). Rob picked him up, hugged him, walked around holding him and knew when to put him down.

They were inseparable. It was funny, wherever Rob went, the little duck was right behind him and a few times, Rob was right behind the baby duck. You can tell the difference between the familiar connection and one of owning a loved pet.

THE DOLPHIN

The Dolphin, whale, porpoise, are in the same family. These are intelligent (they also learn quickly) communicators.

They ride the ocean waves, swim in the vast unknown and are comfortable in it. As with inner vastness within us and the vast universe, we can learn from them by going deep within ourselves.

They are fun loving and active. Dolphins are social and thus like swimming in groups.

They are known for helping each other (as an example when injured). Along the same line, we have all heard how a dolphin helped a person lost or drowning in the water to survive and some have helped to bring a person to safety.

Therefore, they are considered also to be nurturing and protective. These qualities can sometimes create difficulty in a person who doesn't know when to stop taking care of others or when to stop giving. It is a positive trait, but the universe has a balance and you also need to get something back.

THE DRAGON

© **Original Art By Carol Ann Rodriguez**

The dragon energy has been with us for ages. They are known as protectors (of treasures, castles, people, etc.) They are the wise sages who give knowledge and insight into both realms (the physical and non-physical). Therefore, they help you to study and learn in any area of your choice. Dragons also have great strength.

They are also said to be evil, but we are only attracting the positive ancients.

They can also be various elemental types such as Water -West/deals with emotions, Fire-South/energy, sexual energy, Earth-North/property, finance, Air-East/intellect, spirituality. Of course there are more qualities, but you have an idea this way. If you have a dragon as a familiar, it will be very loyal to you.

Story –

My main familiar is a dragon. A friend of mine, Bro. Revels-Bey, was renting a room in a house with other people years ago. He wasn't planning on living there for long because some of the people were negative. He called me up one day and said he's going to New Jersey (we're in NY) because he felt something was "off" and needed to get away. He asked me to make sure his room was safe and nothing would happen to his belongings.

He went on his way and I put my dragon outside his door to guard it.

I got a call the next day that the police were at his house looking for him. It turned out that someone accidentally started a fire and the whole house burned. I got there as soon as I could. The house was all black. There were a few pieces of furniture left and on the lawn that were so burned, it was hard to recognize what they were.

The only room that didn't burn was his. Not one thing burned. The police were looking for him because they thought he might have started the fire since his room strangely wasn't touched by it. Luckily, he could prove he was out of state. He still had to get rid of many things due to the scent of the smoke permeating some items. Dragons are great protectors.

Witchcraft, The Occult And How To Select A Familiar

THE HAWK

The hawk is another strong connection to my people. They are known for their hunting skills. They are invisible to their prey until they attack suddenly. We are known for staying unseen in battle until the arrows and blades come out. (Like a bolt of Lightning.) Now, you know we don't do negative. However, you can utilize these qualities when you are in negotiation in business or in any area of your life. Keep your advantage close to the vest until needed to win.

They have great visual sight and intuitively know when to swoop down on prey (for food). So you can be very observant, focused, see things and notice things others may miss. This also gives you intuitive, psychic insight when you need it and makes you a visionary when you are open to it.

Note that domesticated birds bond easily with us.

ANGELS

Angels, angels everywhere. Some are seen, some are not, but there they are when you need them.

These include archangels. You can invoke them to come to your aid. Make sure you know if it has a specific purpose, since it can only perform to their ability. Otherwise ask that an angel come to you that connects to your cause. (State your cause.) These messengers of the heavenly kingdom want to help us and are happy to do so.

Angels will bring out the best in you. They bring peace, joy, harmony, trust, understanding, aligning within yourself or in connection to nature and of course positive intent. They help in transitional times, are uplifting, healing of body and spirit and so much more. Various people have seen angels in different forms. They are Light beings and come to you the way they feel you'll be comfortable seeing or sensing them since you invoked them. ALWAYS call for a "positive angel" or "angel of Light" if you don't have a specific name. After all, there are negative, dark angels.

THE STONE

These include all minerals and stones. Gemstones, river rocks, pebbles from a mountain, common stones found on the pavement and so forth. You can get more specific information in my book *"Secret Magical Elixirs Of Life."* These stones are part of mother earth and vibrate with palpable energy. Everything in the universe is made up of energy and thus has a vibrational imprint that attracts or repels various situations, beings and people. Examples: apache tear – is grounding and reflection, bloodstone – brings vitality, stops bleeding, increases talents, balances chakras, idealism, turquoise - all-purpose stone, luck, abundance, protection, health, moonstone - love, romance, inspiration, balance emotions, attract loyal friends, pyrite – also called fool's gold, money, opportunity to gain money.

If you see a stone on the street that catches your eye and you are attracted to it, pick it up. It's meant to be yours.

Hold your stone in your hand. Ask it what its purpose is and pay attention to your first thoughts. That will be your answer from your stone familiar.

MOTORCYCLES AND CARS

This totem has to be a surprise…

Now I know most of you don't think of something like a motorcycle or car as a totem, but it can very well be. Just like stones, it has a pull for some people. This includes all forms of vehicles.

Have you ever noticed how some people act around their car or bike? They give them names, make sure they take care of them and identify with them in some manner. Think of someone you know like that, what type of car they have and how it fits them. My parents had racing cars and my mother always named hers. She was just like that car, racing around doing 20 focused things. They had a sense of adventure (which seems to have passed onto my sons too) and a feel for speed. We would go to car races and try to figure out who'd win and which cars attracted us.

The color has meaning too if that's a familiar.

Look at what qualities you have in common and what feelings it gives you if you have a familiar like any of these. What do they represent to you?

THE HIGH ENERGY LEOPARD

This includes those in the cat family, such as: lion, cheetah, tiger, lynx, cat (think of them in nature, in the wild), jaguar and puma, among others.

They have high energy and so are good to invoke when you need that level.

I know when you think of a cat, you're thinking of them laying around, taking their time wandering around the house and being sometimes playful and independent. However, think of cats in the wild. They look relaxed, but when they are on the hunt, get out of their way. They will lay low and then pounce or you can see them run at full speed and attack their prey.

They are powerful, agile, focused (when hunting for food), graceful and cunning.

If you have a familiar in the cat family, some of those traits are yours and you can consciously use them in business or your personal life. If you need help in any of these areas, call in whichever cat you're attracted to.

There are deities connected to cats and the angel Camael can change to a leopard when invoked. So be aware.

137

THE ANCESTORS

Our ancestors are around us to help us any way they can. Ancestors include parents that have passed on. This is NOT mediumship. You never ask for ancestors to come to you by name when you are working with them as familiars.

This is because you may have a purpose that they are not able to help you with and now, not only are you not getting the help needed, but you made your ancestors feel bad that they are unable to provide the help they so much want to give. You don't ask an artist to fix your plumbing.

The way you would phrase calling on them is as follows, say:

I call on my ancestors to help me. I call on my ancestor who has the ability to help me with (say what your intent is). Come to me now through time and space, come to me with ease and grace.

Be aware whether you feel someone or not, your ancestor is there with you. Say thank you for coming, say what you want done again. And tell your ancestor to go forth to help you.

THE HARE

The bunny is very cute so they look vulnerable. Yet they're really not. When a predator is flying overhead, the rabbit cannot gaze upward, but will feel it coming through the photosensitive cells on its back. You can see it running away even when the bird is still too high and farther away. So much for thinking they are actually being too vulnerable.

Their cuteness, up to a point protects them from, as an example, some of us. Their line of defense is to first lay low, if that doesn't work, then they run. It depends on the situation. They are smart animals.

Their senses are extraordinarily developed. And though they like the open spaces, which are usually where we see them, they like to live in smaller, more confined spaces for safety.

Unlucky for them, we consider a rabbit's foot lucky to carry to bring luck to us. We don't believe in harming them. In some places they will use the rabbit for food, as some other animals, but that is different.

The hare is considered in some cultures to be a symbol with sexual connotations because they are prolific.

What qualities do you see that remind you of yourself? What qualities do you need to call in a hare for your intent?

THE CHAMELEON

This animal can camouflage itself automatically to blend in anywhere to survive. They can blend with their environment changing themselves to fit in perfectly. And they always look like wherever they are, they belong there. Interesting traits, don't you think? How can you use these familiar attributes?

The chameleon is an interesting creature. Its ability comes in handy when you want to instantly fit in with any situation or any people, such as, on a new job or at a party, among other situations. You are good at blending in but to be happy, you should stay with the people you fit with the most. Chameleons, as people, are the ones who automatically speak to someone in a way that the person understands, switching automatically from one person to another. Example: if I am speaking to my business clients, I say-it pertains to. If I am speaking to a young guy who often hangs out I will say it differently. I am not speaking "up" or "down," just their way. Blending also makes you a good mediator.

THE FOX

People tend to think of a fox as sly because it doesn't run in a straight line. If it did, the hunter on the horse would surely kill it since the horse is faster. Its survival instinct tells it to avoid threats in this way. It is the survival instinct. The fox is good at diverting an attacker which also takes courage. They are also intelligent, because they see the situation they're in and they take the right action.

If you are walking through the woods and you see a fox near you, it will just keep walking and not bother you. However, if you are near their young, they are very protective and you should run, run, run.

The fox is also family oriented and so his instinct to protect will outweigh its urge for survival.

Do you see any connections to you?

THE PARROT

It is said that parrots are so smart that in order not to be cooked like a chicken or a turkey, they learned the speech of man. They're smart birds, right? So if you have a parrot familiar, you have excellent communication skills and can be good at solving problems.

Since these birds are very social and like to be around other parrots and people, you would enjoy jobs working with others.

These birds have individual personalities. They can be loud; especially when they want attention or are pointing out they need something. Others may be very quiet. Some love to be petted and some can be needy. All of them like attention but in various degrees.

When you look at the baby birds, they look cute and you just want to hold and pet them. When they are older, they may stay the same or be a little aggressive. If you've ever tried to take food from a parrot, you know they can bite you very hard.

THE DOG

There are several types of dogs, and although they may have the same basic qualities, they still have their differences. They come in all shapes. There are tiny dogs up to large dogs. Your familiar and you will be drawn to each other when you have some of the same traits.

They are known to be loyal as long as you treat them well and deserve their loyalty.

Golden Retriever

These dogs are very friendly and love to be part of a family. Although they're also used in hunting to retrieve birds, they are also used for companionship. They are very disciplined and careful. After all, they are bringing the bird right back to the hunter and are careful not to damage it.

They are one of the most loyal dogs and generally are very happy. Hence, you would be family oriented, as they are. You also would be good with friends.

The golden retriever has a high intelligence level and likes to learn.

They are very lovable.

Terrier

They are very adaptable dogs. They can be in open spaces or in small apartments and are happy with either. You would do well in any environment, since adaptability is natural to you if you have this familiar.

They are known for being friendly and good in a family environment. They can be loud at times and intense when they have something they're focused on.

The terrier likes to be top dog. So he can be bossy to gain the role he likes as the dominant dog. In people, these traits would help you attain a leadership position. You wouldn't be good as a quiet follower.

Terriers are very active. Keep that in mind when job hunting. You wouldn't like a sedentary job for too long.

Poodle

The poodle is an elegant and proud looking dog. They are impressive to look at and are frequently in dog shows. This also shows you that they like to learn, since they train rather quickly for the shows. They look regal, don't they?

They are very friendly and don't like to be alone too much. This is not the personality of the loner.

They like to be playful. How playful are you?

Collie

They are very sensitive and highly intelligent dogs.

A collie has a strong sense of loyalty. They will have a keen feel for the need of their owner. With people that would translate into being very aware of what people close to you need.

They are known to have an affectionate nature. Although they are usually not loud, they can be if there is a reason.

As people, they like to be louder at times to get their point across.

Beagle

Beagles are very active, fun dogs. They like to run and play. But they are hounds and can be independent and stubborn at times.

They are cute, gentle and lovable and like to be around people. However, if alone for too long, they can get bored easily. As a person, you would look for ways to be active to counteract the boredom.

A beagle will focus on something and follow that interest until he/she finds out what or where it is.

Back to dogs in general:

As you can see, not all dogs are the same. Are there traits that fit you? Are there traits that you'd like to have? If you have a dog or had a dog in the past, look at his/her qualities to see which ones match you. After all, if you resonate with the energies of your dog, you must have some common ground. Check to see what they are. It will tell you a little about yourself.

Diane Tessman with Hannah, one of her favorite familiars.
www.earthchangepredictions.com

THE CAT

There are several breeds of cats. Some traits carry through all of them such as being independent, cunning, hunters, agile, resourceful and having their own personalities. Let's look at some and see if you have anything in common with them.

Cats have been known as familiars for centuries. Think of how much the Egyptians were focused on them in several varied forms. Cats are associated with witches, sorcerers, oracles and magi and others.

The witch is known for acquiring a physical cat to send out to do her bidding and return to her. Some say that she pulls in a spirit to reside inside the cat body for her to control. Some say her spirit can go into the body of the cat at will and perform her magick. Others say she controls the cat with her witchcraft. While others say that she controls the spirit of a cat, not the physical being.

Some worship a cat deity to help in times of trouble or to better a situation. We only work the positive side of magick with our familiars.

You may or may not resonate to a cat familiar. If you do, you will be following in the footsteps of many light workers. If you don't feel an affinity to a cat, you will resonate with a familiar that is better for you.

Remember, you can always call in a familiar for a specific purpose that is not your particular connection.

Siamese

This cat has a very distinctive look and a high level of intelligence.

They can be very vocal which means a person can be good at expressing an idea or a point of view. This can be a bonus. These cats love attention and being around people.

Siamese cats are very active. If you want a quiet, docile cat, this is not the one.

They can carry themselves with grace.

Another trait for the Siamese cat is being very persistent. Do you have this trait?

Persian

It's funny how you can look at a Persian cat and think how fluffy it looks.

Now, this is a quiet cat, unlike the Siamese cat. It just wants to roam around.

The Persian cat likes affection and will come to you for that feeling of being touched, but only when it wants to. It is a mood, after all.

Being inquisitive is another trait.

Alley Cat

Now, this is a very different type of cat.

This one is more of a hunter (for food). This calls for the ability to be agile and cunning. The Alley cat is a survivor in all sense of that word.

Alley cats will fight when they need to keep what is theirs or for something they need, such as fighting over food.

They are intelligent and very resourceful.

These cats are loners, but will be protective over their family if they have one.

Do you see yourself in this role? Can you utilize some of these abilities when a situation might call for it?

Calico

These cats have mixed colors. It's interesting how you'll never see two looking the same.

They are feisty, precocious and intelligent.

Calico cats are very independent. They like their space. Yet they are very loyal.

These cats are very loving, so if you like to have unconditional love, this is the cat for you.

Back to cats in general:

Cats show a high level of confidence and don't like to be restricted in their movements. They can be very spontaneous.

Do you resonate with cats? What part of your personality matches with them? What part doesn't? This will give you insight about yourself.

Prayer for Power

I am one with God
   and let the power of God
      flow in me,
         through me,
            and around me,
For God is All.
I trust the Divine Power
      and all is perfect
Knowing I am always protected
      and guided Divinely.
Whatever I choose
      to manifest in my life
         comes easy to me,
Joyfully and with perfect harmony.

I walk the path of White Light
      in Truth,   Peace,
            Love,
               Harmony and Health.
Thank you Father for I am,
      You are,
         We are ONE.

               Amen.
by Rev. Maria D'Andrea

CONCLUSION

Feel better and happier because you are raising your vibration. The more you work with spiritual energies and your familiars, the higher your vibration gets automatically.

The vibration of this planet is about 100,000 vibrations per second. When, as an example, a healer is working with healing energy, the vibration of the healer raises to that of the earth. When the healer is finished, it just goes back down to the healers' natural level. Mankind vibrates lower. We are working on gaining enlightenment, thus rising to match our planet's vibes.

We create by focusing our thoughts and being positive with our feelings so Divine Power can respond to us. So when you are feeling good, you are raising your vibration. Simpler than you thought? Keep this attitude.

You already know what you need to know. Spread your wings and let yourself fly high. Your Source doesn't limit you, so why would you? Once you make up your mind to fly, you'll take off.

It is all in the knowledge, effort, positivity and knowing. Be aware of what is coming from your heart and your spirit.

Let yourself get in the streaming energy and be YOU. Do you think Einstein, Tesla, Picasso and others went by the rules of society all the time? Of course not. We wouldn't have art and all the wonders we have today. Go Rock That Boat.

When you have problems, get up! Stay up! Keep moving forward...Give yourself credit, because you (and your familiar) are doing great. You only fail if you do nothing. If something doesn't work, it's ok. Learn and keep moving with a smile. Be happy, you just learned something. Plus the universe is attracted to positivity, laughter and humor. I am telling you, some days I think I actually hear the universe laughing at me.

Get excited about your future. It is already in you.

My son, Rick came up with this: instead of the GPS which helps us get directions to navigate and get to our destination, he said we have a "PPS"© = *Psychic Positioning System*. My other son Rob added the G. So now we have "GPPS"© = *Global Psychic Positioning System*. How great is it that we can navigate on both realities?

I believe in you. Go forth and create your world.

YES YOU CAN!!!

SOME OTHER BOOKS (Partial List)
BY MARIA D'ANDREA   MsD, D.D., DRH

The Complete Magickal, Spiritual And Occult Oils Workbook
From A-Z

Heaven Sent Money Spells

Maria D'Andrea's Secret Occult Gallery And Spell Casting
Formulary

How To Eliminate Stress And Anxiety Through The Occult

Maria D'Andrea's Simple Spells With Playing Cards

Occult Grimoire And Magical Formulary

100% Positive Spells And Incantations For Aladdin's Magick
Lamp

Yes You Can Series:

The Sexy Medium's Love And Lust Spells

Supernatural Words Of Power

Travel The Waves Of Time Contacting Beneficial Beings

Evocation

Maria D'Andrea's Book Of Common Prayer

Maria D'Andrea's Your Personal Mega Power Spells

Secret Magical Elixirs Of Life

Co-authored or Contributed:

Maria D'Andrea's Positively Positive Spell Book

Angel Spells

Maria D'Andrea's Mythical, Magickal Beasts And Beings

Witchcraft, The Occult And How To Select A Familiar

Curses And Their Reverses

The Pyramids Speak

Timothy Green Beckley's Amityville And Beyond

A Miracle A Minute

The Ark Of The Covenant

Miracle Candle Spells

The Matrix Control System Of Philip K. Dick And The Paranormal Synchronicities Of Timothy Green Beckley

DVD Sets (Partial List):

3 DVD Set-Maria D'Andrea's Spiritual Life Counseling

The Power OF Planting Spiritual Seeds; You Can Live A Shamanic

Life; Developing The Healer Within

3 DVD Set-Series #2 Maria D'Andrea's Spiritual Life Counseling

Attracting Relationships; Surrender Yourself To A Positive Life;

Angels And The Fall

Write for our FREE catalog of amazing books and other fascinating items.

INNER LIGHT/GLOBAL COMMUNICATIONS

P.O. Box 753
New Brunswick, NJ 08903

mrufo8@hotmail.com

Made in the USA
Columbia, SC
04 August 2020